United Tastes of America

Dorinda Hafner

Book and Chapter Introductions
by Sue Shephard

EBURY PRESS
LONDON

First published in 1997

1 3 5 7 9 10 8 6 4 2

Text © Dorinda Hafner 1997
Photographs © Individual photographers 1997

First published in the United Kingdom in 1997 by Ebury Press
Random House, 20 Vauxhall Bridge Road, London SW1V 2SA

Random House Australia (Pty) Limited
20 Alfred Street, Milsons Point, Sydney,
New South Wales 2061, Australia

Random House New Zealand Limited
18 Poland Road, Glenfield, Auckland 10, New Zealand

Random House South Africa (Pty) Limited
Endulini, 5a Jubilee Road, Parktown 2193, South Africa

Random House UK Limited Reg. No. 954009

Papers used by Ebury Press are natural, recyclable products made from wood grown
in sustainable forests.

A CIP catalogue record for this book is available from the British Library.

ISBN 0 09 185415 6

Designed by Geoff Hayes
Jacket design by Alison Shackleton
Front cover photography by Simon Farrell © Ebury Press
Front cover styling by Tag Lamche and Lucy Miller
Food photography by Milton Wordley
Food styling by Catherine Kerry
Location photography by Cassie Farrell, Nicola Colton and Valerie Haselton

Printed and bound in the UK by Butler and Tanner Ltd, Frome, Somerset

'United Tastes of America' is a Harvest Entertainment production for Channel 4

Contents

Introduction   4

Further reading   6

Cajun American Tastes   7

African American Tastes 23

Chinese American Tastes 40

German American Tastes 56

Italian American Tastes   72

Jewish American Tastes   88

New Mexican Tastes   107

Native American Tastes   125

Index   143

Introduction

America is the land of plenty – plenty of food, in particular. Food is an integral part of the history of the USA, and the story of America and its 'united tastes' is long and full of pain and hardship.

No-one can be quite sure which foreigners first set foot on the shores of the New World. One thing is quite certain – the indigenous Indians, or Native Americans, already enjoyed a rich natural larder, which they hunted and cultivated with great skill and sophistication. There were deer, elk, moose and bear, also hares, rabbits, squirrels, waterfowl, grouse, quail, woodcock and that now most famous of all American native birds, the turkey. There were countless varieties of fish in the lakes and seas, not to mention shellfish such as crabs, oysters, crawfish, lobster and clams. Native Americans knew how to cultivate corn, beans and squash, the staples of their diet. They also grew peas, pumpkins, melons, sunflowers, chillies and bell peppers. They gathered wild fruits and berries, herbs, mushrooms, roots and nuts such as cranberries, strawberries, whortleberries, peanuts, hickory, pecans and beechnuts and they sweetened their food with wild honey and maple syrup.

Perhaps the greatest, most important gift from Native Americans to modern American cuisine is corn. The Native American had learned by trial and error how to grow a staple food that would eventually feed a nation. All across the United States, corn is the basis of delicious classic dishes from simple buttery corn on the cob to cornflakes, tortillas, cornbread, grits, cornmeal mush, posole and many others, not forgetting, of course, that now universal favourite snack, popcorn.

Over the centuries, numerous and varied waves of people have come ashore along the coasts of America. Some came more willingly than others. Many had no choice in the matter. Americans today are proud and protective of their regional cuisines, whose origins go back over the centuries in a blending of dishes and ingredients into a great patchwork of culinary delights. Some people may tell you that American food today is bland, mass-produced and unhealthy. Well, they don't know where to look or how to find the best places for regional specialities. Regional cuisines are created by the mix of people and their past, as well as by climate and local ingredients.

In New England and along the East Coast, traditional American cooking first started to develop. This reflected not just the simple Puritan religion of the first settlers but also their need to cook nutritious, warming food to get them through the long, cold winters. Puddings both sweet and savoury and stews cooked slowly in huge pots hung over fires that, with the plentiful firewood, could be kept burning all day, were examples of the northern European traditions. There was also the rich harvest of fish in the North Atlantic such as cod and herring as well as coastal lobsters and oysters brought in by Portuguese, Italian and English fishermen which gave us seafood chowders, pickled herring, gefilte fish and many other delicious fish dishes.

The Mid-West and North-West regions, also known as the 'heartland' and the 'breadbasket' of America, include rich dairy and stock farmlands and endless prairies of tall, waving cereals. Huge breakfasts and hearty meals in the German, Slavic and Scandinavian tradition are needed to fuel long days of hard work on the farms. This is the home of bratwurst, beer, pickles and dairy foods, as well as potatoes and apples, brought together with the maple syrup, cranberries, wild rice and fish from Native American traditions.

In the South-West, which includes New Mexico, Arizona, California and Texas, there are hot, fierce looking landscapes reminiscent of huge ranches, with cowboys or gauchos eating burritos with refried beans and riding the range. Here an extraordinary mix of Spanish, Mexican, Native American (Pueblo and Navajo) and Anglos have combined a range of specialities from chiles rellenos, posole and chili con carne, to regional cuisines including the popular American hybrid Tex Mex and the more authentic New Mexican. On the South-West coast of California are exotic Asian and Mediterranean traditions, Chinese and other Oriental ingredients with their quick cooking to stay cool and healthy, salads of local fresh produce, and delicious fish from the warm ocean waters for rich Italian stews.

The Southern states are famous for their hospitality and their cuisine, with its roots firmly in three distinct cultures, English, French and African plus, as ever, local Native American influence. Traditional southern food stems from nineteenth-century English and French cuisines, reinterpreted by early African American cooks who brought with them the cooking traditions of Africa and the Caribbean. Southern cooking features ingredients such as okra, eggplant, black-eyed peas, coconut, sugar, rum, chocolate and tropical fruits; cakes and desserts in the English tradition; open-air cooking and barbecues, and plenty of ice-cold drinks. The now famous soul food is a form of African American cultural expression which grew out of the necessity to produce palatable food from the poorest cuts and most meagre ingredients available to them.

Last, but certainly not least in the Southern states is Cajun cuisine – an amazing story of French regional cooking on the run in the mangrove swamps of the Mississippi, where it merged with Native American hunting and fishing skills, resulting in local wildlife cooked and 'smothered' in sauces from Picardy.

For later immigrants, to become a true American, to taste and enjoy the new world's fruits, was the dream. Sadly, arrival in America was often followed by a long and painful period of adjustment and cultural self-denial. The association with one's ethnicity was of ignorance and poverty; assimilation meant rejecting the past and embracing the English-speaking, homogenous, all-American society where the wonderful potential for a multi-cultural melting pot of flavours and aromas was thrown over in favour of fast foods, convenience ingredients and fashionable 'smart foods'. The love affair with beef, wheat and dairy products all eaten in vast quantities looked like lasting for a long time. Nevertheless the hamburger, hot dog, Chicago pizza, chop suey, cioppina and chili con carne emerged as popular foods inspired by 'foreign' cultures. Little by little, the genuine immigrant foods became more acceptable. People got used to the tastes and aromas of garlic, chillies, olives and strong cheeses. The advent of international travel and the inevitable development of closer contact and intermarriage with other ethnic groups led to greater tolerance of different lifestyles and different food. Neighbours, schoolmates and fellow workers were introduced by immigrants to German, Jewish, Hungarian, Chinese, Mexican and Italian restaurants where they discovered the delights of exciting new dishes such as home made pasta, turkey mole, dim sum, pastrami, jambalaya and strudel. The fact that most Americans who enjoy eating out nowadays choose first between Italian, Chinese, Mexican and many other ethnic restaurants is testament to how far they have come on the journey to United Tastes!

As George Meredith once said: 'Kissing don't last ... cookery do.' Enjoy!

Bibliography and **Further** Reading

GENERAL

Lesley Allin, *Great American Food*. Rosendale Press: London, 1994.

American Heritage Cookbook. American Heritage Publishing Ltd: 1964 (OP).

Betty Fussell, *I Hear America Cooking*. Elizabeth Sifton Books/Viking:New York, 1986.

Heritage of America Cookbook. Better Homes and Gardens Books: Iowa, 1993.

Evan Jones, *American Food*. The Overlook Press: New York, 1990.

Elizabeth Rozin, *Blue Corn and Chocolate*. Ebury Press: London, 1992.

AFRICAN AMERICAN TASTES

Eric V. Copage, *Kwanzaa: An African-American Celebration of Culture and Cooking*. William Morrow & Co., Inc.: New York, 1991.

John Egerton, *Southern Food: At Home, On the Road, In History*. University of North Carolina Press, 1993.

Damon Lee Fowler, *Classical Southern Cooking*. Crown Publishers: New York, 1995.

Karen Hess, *The Carolina Rice Kitchen: The African Connection*. University of South Carolina Press, 1992.

JEWISH AMERICAN TASTES

Gil Marks, *The World of Jewish Cooking*. Simon & Schuster: New York, 1996.

Joan Nathan, *Jewish Cooking in America*. Alfred A. Knopf: New York, 1995.

Claudia Roden, *The Book of Jewish Food*. Alfred A.Knopf: New York, 1996.

Raymond Sokolov, *The Jewish American Kitchen*. Wings Books: New York, 1989.

CAJUN AMERICAN TASTES

Barry Jean Ancelot, Jay Edwards and Glen Pitre, *Cajun Country*. University Press of Mississippi: 1991

C.Paige Gutierrez, *Cajun Foodways*. University Press of Mississippi: 1992

Emeril Lagasse, *Louisiana Real and Rustic*. William Morrow and Co., Inc.: New York, 1996.

The Prudhomme Family, *The Prudhomme Family Cookbook*. William M

CHINESE AMERICAN TASTES

Shirley Fong-Torres, *In the Chinese Kitchen*. Pacific View Press: Berkeley, CA, 1993.

—— *San Francisco Chinatown: A Walking Tour*. China Books: San Francisco, 1991.

Frances Bissell, *Oriental Flavours*. Macmillan: London, 1990.

Barbara Tropp, *The Modern Art of Chinese Cooking: Techniques and Recipes*. Hearst Books, New York: 1982.

NEW MEXICAN TASTES

Cheryl Alters Jamison & Bill Jamison, *The Border Cookbook*. Harvard Common Press: Harvard, 1995.

Lynn Nusom, *The Sizzling Southwestern Cookbook*. Lowell House: Los Angeles, 1996.

GERMAN AMERICAN TASTES

Marcia Adams, Heartland: *The Best of the Old and the New from Midwest Kitchens*. Clarkson Potter: New York, 1991.

NATIVE AMERICAN TASTES

Beverly Cox and Martin Jacobs, *Spirit of the Harvest: North American Indian Cooking*. Stewart Tabori & Chang: New York, 1991.

Frances Densmore, *Chippewa Customs*. Minnesota Historical Society Press, 1979.

ITALIAN AMERICAN TASTES

Antonion Carluccio, *Antonio Carluccio's Italian Feast*. BBC Books: London, 1996.

Julia Della Croce. *Pasta Classica*. Chronicle Books: San Francisco, 1996.

Mary Ann Esposito, *Celebration Italian Style*. Hearst Books: New York, 1995.

If you are interested in a particular ethnic taste and would like to find more of their recipes it is always worth going to bookshops, libraries and information bureaux in the region or community where you will often find home produced and printed booklets of recipes written by local people themselves. For example, in Gloucester, Mass., I found a wonderful little book of fish recipes by Italian American fishermen's wives and in New Ulm, Minnesota, I obtained a very useful little collection of German American recipes recorded by members of the community.

Cajun American Tastes

Of all the communities I have met in America, the Cajuns have probably the most extraordinary story. They were among the first European settlers to develop a sense of identity separate from their country of origin, and they have created a unique culture that has evolved since they settled in the swamps and bayous of the Mississippi and the southwestern prairies of Louisiana.

The beautiful and distinct French colonial architecture of New Orleans is a reminder of the long period of French settlement and cultural influence in this area. Slaves from West Africa and the Caribbean were imported to work the large farms and plantations. The word Creole, also the name for another famous cuisine in the area, was given to people born in the colony of Louisiana. This included people of French, Spanish, African and mixed parentage, who were born in Louisiana, to distinguish them from European immigrants still arriving, as well as Africans still being brought through the slave routes. Originally, Creole meant simply, "local, home grown, not imported", and it referred not only to people and things but ways of doing things – including cooking.

Many people confuse Creole cuisine with Cajun, and there are indeed some things they do have in common, including some classic dishes such as gumbo. When loosely defined, Creole cooking is city cooking originating in Louisiana, and Cajun cooking is country cooking of Acadian origins.

In the mid 18th century, France ceded Louisiana to Spain, who used the colony as a barrier to protect its vast gold and silver mines in Mexico and the southwest against the threat from Anglo-American settlements to the north and east. Immigrants from many countries were encouraged to settle, but the single largest group were the Acadians, people of French origin who had settled in the then French colony of Nova Scotia as early as 1632. In 1755 the British captured the colony and ordered the Acadians (or Cadians) to take an oath of allegiance or be expelled. Many escaped and spread through Canada, America and the Caribbean. The offer of land, albeit poor land, and some assistance from the Spanish in Louisiana must have seemed a godsend. Word spread, and over the years the Acadians slowly moved into the swamps, prairies and coastal regions, where they started to rebuild their lives. A strong sense of family and community fortified these fragmented people as they struggled to survive as a

'Junior' with his 'turkduckhens'

group. But they also lived alongside and intermarried with settlers from other European countries as well as the Native American tribes and some African Creoles. An inevitable blending of cultures produced what we now know as the Cajuns – a mispronunciation of Cadians.

The story of Cajun cuisine is particularly fascinating. The Acadians first originated in the Poitou region of France – an area still famous for its distinct French provincial cuisine. The French art of sauce-making, or roux, is central to Cajun cooking. Marinades, spices and long slow cooking in casseroles are all from traditional French provincial cuisine, originally developed by country people to stretch simple poor food and make it more palatable. The Cajun boudin sausages, both red and white, are derived from the original French boudin noir or blood sausage. Andouille, stuffed large intestines, and chaudin, stuffed stomach, along with fromage de tête, head cheese, are all part of the tradition of using every part of the animal when it is butchered. Cajun cuisine, however, would probably be unrecognizable today to a visitor from France. The famous gumbo has clear African origins, and the equally renowned sauce piquante using hot peppers, spices and tomatoes has Spanish and African Caribbean sources.

When the Acadians re-located from the cold north of Nova Scotia to subtropical Louisiana, they had to learn many new things, including what was available to eat and how to cook it. The prairie settlers established ranches and developed dykes to reclaim some of the low coastal land. The local Native Americans taught them how to fish bass, catfish, perch and crawfish in the bayous, and how to hunt alligator, possum, wild turkey, raccoon, squirrel, elk, moose and other game. They learned how to cultivate corn, potatoes, beans and rice, while the French and African Creoles taught them how to grow sugar cane, okra and cotton. They soon established self-sufficient farms for their large families, and many Cajuns today still keep a close attachment to the land – fishing, hunting and camping out on the banks of the bayous.

Crawfish is probably the food most often associated with Cajun cuisine, although it has only become popular fairly recently. A crawfish boil (see p.13) is a hugely popular family event, with hundreds of fresh crawfish rapidly boiled in a large vat with potatoes, corn, vegetables and spices, then tipped onto a table covered in newspaper. Cajun culture and Cajun cuisine have adapted to changing times, their cooking continues to evolve, and at the same time it has become enormously popular and commercial. All over the world you can buy pre-blended "Cajun" spices and frozen "Cajun" meals, and eat "Cajun" dishes in smart restaurants in Sydney, New York, London and Paris. An extraordinary journey for a cuisine and its people who, it is said, "live to eat rather than eat to live".

Dorinda writes:
"My Cajun friends jokingly said of their food, 'We'll eat anything that does not eat us first!'. Cajuns are ingenious in adapting to their environment. Survival is the name of the game, and Cajuns have played it to win. Early Cajun meals were designed by necessity to be economical. One-pot cooking became very popular, using ingredients which by themselves would go nowhere, but in Cajun hands would be transformed with herbs and spicy seasonings into a variety of mouthwatering treats. Cajun food is a blend of spicy, tasty wholesome country cooking. An invitation to eat Cajun is a chance to sit at nature's table and be filled with culinary surprises. When I think Cajun, I think gumbo, crawfish, boudin, jambalaya, rice, andouille, garlic, cayenne pepper – and other exotica."

Dorinda's Cajun Combo Seasoning Mix

Today, many who cook "Cajun" use an assortment of bought "Cajun" spices. I think if you can make time to put together your own Cajun spices, do it. At least you'll know what you're eating. This, then, is my Cajun combo seasoning.

Dry Version

4 tablespoons paprika

4 tablespoons onion powder

4 tablespoons dried thyme

2 tablespoons dried oregano

I tablespoon cayenne pepper

6 teaspoons freshly ground black pepper

6 teaspoons freshly ground white pepper

4 teaspoons celery salt

4 teaspoons garlic salt

3 teaspoons garlic powder

Fresh Version

I large red pepper, de-seeded and very finely chopped

I large red onion, peeled and very finely chopped

4 tablespoons chopped fresh thyme

3 tablespoons chopped fresh oregano

2–3 teaspoons fresh chillies, very finely chopped

4 teaspoons finely chopped fresh leafy celery tops

2 garlic cloves, peeled and finely chopped

6 teaspoons freshly ground black pepper

6 teaspoons freshly ground white pepper

3 heaped teaspoons sea salt

For either version, mix all the ingredients together in a screw-top glass jar. Store until needed. The dry version can be kept in the jar for up to 6 months unrefrigerated, or up to 1 year in a refrigerator. The fresh version must be stored in a refrigerator, for up to 3 days only.

Note: For the fresh version, deseed the fresh chillies if you don't want it too hot.

Corn and Crab Bisque

SERVES 4–6

When the Cajuns first arrived in the bayou country of Louisiana in the mid 18th century, the terrain was harsh, but they learnt very quickly how to survive, what to hunt and what to eat – and none was more helpful than the Native American tribes of the region, the Houmas, the Chitimaca and others. They taught the Cajuns about local produce, including wild corn and river crabs. The French Cajuns added their culinary know-how and a handsome soup was born of native American and Cajun parents. Now this baby is busy winning medals in competitions.

125 g/4 oz butter

375 g/12 oz sweetcorn kernels

I onion, peeled and finely chopped

3 garlic cloves, peeled and finely chopped

I green pepper (capsicum), de-seeded and finely chopped

I celery stick, finely chopped

125 g/4 oz plain flour

1.5 litres/3 pints seafood stock (see below)

125 ml/4 fl oz thick cream

250 g/8 oz crabmeat, from the body

250 g/8 oz crabmeat, from the claws

a handful of chopped chives, spring onion

tops, fresh thyme or parsley, to garnish

Melt the butter in a large saucepan and sauté the sweetcorn, onion, garlic, pepper and celery for about 10 minutes until the vegetables are cooked. Make your roux by adding the flour to the vegetables and butter. Cook on low heat until well blended but not browned. Carefully stir in the seafood stock until well mixed, then bring to a boil and cook on high for 5 minutes. Lower the heat and simmer for 30 minutes.

Stir in first the cream, then the crabmeats, taking care not to stir too vigorously or the crabmeats will break up. Taste and adjust the seasoning. Continue to cook on low heat for another 10 minutes. Serve hot, garnished with chopped greens like chives, spring onion tops, fresh thyme or parsley.

Seafood Stock

Put 250g/8oz each of prawn, crab and crawfish shells in a large stockpot, together with 1 onion, 1 carrot, 1 celery stick and 3 garlic cloves (quartered), 2 bay leaves, 4 black peppercorns, the rind of 1 lemon, 1 sprig each fresh parsley and basil, 3 glasses of dry white wine and 2 litres/4 pints of water. Bring to the boil and boil for 1 hour. Strain, discard all solids, then return the stock to the stockpot over a low heat. Simmer for a further 30 minutes and use as required.

Chicken and Andouille Sausage Gumbo

SERVES 6–8

Gumbo is a generic name for either a thick soup or a thin stew from south Louisiana. It is usually made up of a seasoned mix of two or more types of seafood, meat and spicy sausage in a roux-based sauce. This Seafood and Andouille Sausage Gumbo is a speciality of Gigi Patout, the diminutive but dynamic Cajun chef at Patout's, her restaurant in St Louis Street, French Quarter, New Orleans.

2 litres/4 pints water

1 kg/2 lb chicken (use thighs, drumsticks and wings for maximum taste)

1 celery stick with leaves, very finely chopped

3 garlic cloves, peeled and finely chopped

2 bay leaves

salt

250 ml/8 fl oz vegetable oil or 250 g/8 oz butter

250 g/8 oz plain flour

2 large onions, peeled and finely chopped

2 peppers (capsicums), de-seeded and finely chopped

375 g/12 oz andouille sausage (spicy Cajun lean pork sausage) or their smoked spicy sausage, sliced into thin rounds

1 tablespoon finely chopped spring onion tops or fresh parsley, to garnish

1 kg/2 lb long-grain rice (preferably aromatic), boiled and hot, to serve

For the Cajun seasoning:

1 teaspoon each of cayenne pepper, garlic powder and filé powder

1/2 teaspoon each of freshly ground black pepper, and freshly ground white pepper

Bring the water to a boil in a large stock pot. Add the chicken, celery, garlic, bay leaves and 1 teaspoon salt and continue boiling for about 40 minutes to 1 hour until the chicken is soft and cooked. Remove the bay leaves and chicken pieces from the chicken stock, and lower the heat under the stock. De-bone the chicken, cut it into medium pieces and set aside. Discard the bay leaves.

Make a roux by heating up the oil or butter in a heavy-based skillet or frying pan. Using a wire whisk, stir in the flour. Lower the heat and keep stirring until the flour turns an even dark golden brown. This will take about 5–10 minutes on medium to low heat. Be careful not to burn the roux or you will have to discard it and start again – a burnt roux will give the dish a bitter taste.

When ready, add the roux to the boiling stock along with the onions, peppers, Cajun seasoning and sausage. Lower the heat and allow to simmer for about 40 minutes before you add the chopped chicken. Taste and adjust seasoning. Simmer for a further 20 minutes, adding more stock if necessary. Serve your gumbo hot, with a sprinkling of chopped onion tops or parsley, and hot boiled rice.

Gumbo

The famous gumbo is a case of "many cooks make recipe work". Arguments abound as to its origins – is it based on the French bouillabaisse and court bouillon of New Orleans, or the African gumbo or okra? Gumbo has drawn on many cultural traditions to become as identified with Cajun cuisine as crawfish. Although okra, called gumbo, from West Africa was originally the main ingredient, there are now as many permutations of gumbo as the human imagination allows. Gumbo cooked with okra is called gumbo févi and gumbo cooked with a roux base and thickened with powdered sassafras leaves is called gumbo filé.

Alligator Piquante

SERVES 4–6

I had the good fortune to be invited to a Cajun men's camp in the Atchafalaya basin – what an eye-opener! The men hunted, chatted in French, served moonshine, played the accordion and cooked this delicious alligator piquante and rice. I ate my first alligator with my first moonshine and I was a goner, the serene setting, the music, the men and the alligator. It was simply heaven. This is the recipe the mayor of Hendersen, nicknamed Monsieur "Two Bit", and his friends cooked for me that wonderful day. And just for your information, I am told that 90–120 cm/3–4 foot alligators yield the best meat!

1 kg/2 lb alligator tail meat

salt to taste

4 teaspoons cayenne pepper

125 ml/4 fl oz vegetable oil

2 tablespoons plain flour

2 large onions, peeled and coarsely chopped

4 garlic cloves, peeled and finely chopped

1 large pepper (capsicum), de-seeded and chopped

375 g/12 oz tomatoes, blanched, peeled and chopped

1 tablespoon tomato purée mixed with 250 ml/8 fl oz water, or 250 ml/8 fl oz tomato sauce

1 tablespoon wine vinegar or fresh lemon juice

1/2 glass of red wine

2 teaspoons caster sugar

4 tablespoons chopped spring onion tops or fresh parsley

1 kg/2 lb rice, boiled and hot, to serve

Cut the meat into 5 cm/2 inch pieces, liberally season it with some salt and half the cayenne pepper, cover and set aside.

In a large saucepan, heat up the oil, stir in the flour and cook on low heat until the flour turns a light golden brown, about 3–4 minutes. Add the onions, garlic and pepper and continue cooking for another 4–5 minutes, stirring regularly until the vegetables are soft and cooked. Add the remaining cayenne, the tomatoes, tomato purée and water or tomato sauce, the vinegar or lemon juice, wine, sugar and half the chopped spring onion tops or parsley.

Simmer for 15–20 minutes, then add the pieces of seasoned meat, making sure they are well covered with sauce. Cook for another 30 minutes or until the meat is tender and soft. Chicken cooks more quickly (see Variations), but alligator and crocodile meat sometimes take longer to cook and may need another 20 minutes or more. When ready, serve with hot rice and garnish with the remaining chopped spring onion tops or parsley.

Variations

You can use crocodile meat if you can't get alligator. If you are squeamish about reptile meat, then substitute chicken breast meat, but bear in mind you lose out on a specific taste and on Cajun authenticity.
You may prefer to skewer your pieces of alligator, crocodile or chicken meat and cook it as kebabs or kebobs. In that case, cut the meat into smaller pieces before you season, and thread the pieces onto wooden skewers previously soaked in water for an hour and wiped clean with a little oil. Cook on the barbecue or under the grill for about 7–10 minutes until tender and well-cooked, then pour the cooked sauce over the meat. You can also add 250 g/8 oz button mushrooms if you wish.

Crawfish Boil

SERVES 4–6

As Gutierrez puts it in his *Cajun Foodways*, "A crawfish boil is an event which celebrates Cajun joie de vivre and ésprit de corps". It is a typical Cajun gathering where the cooks, who are usually men, prepare mountains of crawfish for communal consumption by family, friends or colleagues.

The sheer joy of descending on the boiled beasts with bare hands without recourse to rank or status! The shared intimacy between man and beast and man and man whilst standing or sitting neck to neck, peeling, pinching and sucking – with none of the usual territorial rights at dinner tables – all adds to the excitement of the occasion.

My first crawfish boil was an unforgettable experience in Eunice, a small town just outside Lafayette. I was a guest of Widley and Doris Herbert (pronounced Hay-bear), otherwise affectionately known as the "Soops", and their large extended family. It was THE Cajun experience I had to have. There was plenty of newspaper and crawfish, plenty of hands, laughs, music, plenty of everything. I was told, "Pinch the tail and suck the head, that's the way to eat crawfish". You eat till you burst!

In this recipe I have reduced the usual volume and quantities to make it possible to prepare in the confines of a family kitchen should you so desire.

8 litres/ 8 quarts water

1 tablespoon rock salt

3 large onions, unpeeled and cut horizontally in half

1 large head of garlic, unpeeled and cut horizontally in half

3 lemons, unpeeled and cut horizontally in half

10–12 small red-skinned potatoes

125 g/4 oz ground cayenne powder

1 large bunch of fresh coriander

2 whole peppers (capsicums)

3–4 whole ears of sweetcorn, leaves and silks discarded

5–7 kg/10–14 lb crawfish, crabs, prawns or any crustacean of your choice

In a giant cooking pot, boil the water. Mix together all the ingredients for the seasoning mix (see overleaf), then add to the boiling water with the salt. Wait 2–3 minutes for it to mix with the water, then add the onions, garlic, lemons, potatoes, cayenne pepper, coriander and whole peppers. Stir to mix, then boil on medium heat for 20 minutes.

Divide each ear of sweetcorn horizontally into two or three depending on how big you like your corn. Add the corn to the boil, followed by the crawfish or other crustaceans. Using a long-handled spoon, re-arrange all the pieces in the pot to ensure even cooking, taste the boiling water and adjust the seasoning. Half cover and boil for 5 minutes. Turn off the heat, fully cover the pot and leave to stand for 15–20 minutes.

Prepare your table for serving by lining the top with heaps of open sheets of newspaper. Drain off all the water from the boil and pour the remaining contents directly onto the newspapers on the table. Invite your guests to tuck in! As you and your guests eat, push discarded shells and debris to one side, and let nothing stop your voracious enjoyment of your crawfish boil.

For the seasoning mix:

125 g/4 oz paprika

60 g/2 oz each celery salt and mustard powder

2 teaspoons ground allspice

I teaspoon whole cloves

6 bay leaves

> ### Crawfish
> Crawfish used to be called "mud bugs", a derogatory term in reference to their status as poor Southern fare. With the advent of commercial processing, crawfish have taken on an exotic aura, and become increasingly fashionable to serve at trendy dinner tables. Over eighty per cent of the annual harvest of crawfish is consumed locally. Crawfish has come to symbolize Cajun culture.

Blackened Fish

SERVES 4–6

A true Cajun speciality catapulted onto culinary centre stage by the great Paul Prudhomme. It is easy to cook, and has now become de rigeur on most international menus.

When choosing the fish, make sure the thickness is even. If the fillets are tapered too thinly at the ends, this will make for uneven cooking: the ends will cook too quickly, dry out and may even burn before the rest of the fish is ready.

6 large catfish or other white fish fillets

180 g/6 oz butter, melted and warm

3 tablespoons dry Cajun seasoning mix (page 9)

sprigs of fresh parsley, coriander or oregano, to garnish

6 lemon wedges, to serve

Brush the fillets of fish all over with the warm melted butter.
Using your fingers, smear each fillet generously with the seasoning mix.

Place a non-stick skillet or heavy-based frying pan on medium heat and heat until hot. Place one or two seasoned fish fillets in the hot pan without oil and cook "dry", turning them over to cook both sides until their surfaces blacken. If necessary, add very small portions of the butter to aid the blackening process. When all the fish is cooked through and blackened or charred on each side, heat through any remaining butter and pour it over the top of the fish.

Top with a garnish of your favourite fresh green herb and serve hot, with lemon wedges. You can also serve a side dish of hot boiled rice.

Phyllis's Jambalaya

SERVES 4–6

Phyllis Villien belongs to the Herbert family. It is a big Cajun family, who run a local family restaurant called "Soops", so she is used to cooking for large numbers. Phyllis and I were ensconced in her kitchen cooking jambalaya when her husband David drove at some speed into their driveway in his Ford truck. It appeared he was in a bad mood. He shot out of the truck, strutted around inspecting everything, gave us a "drop-dead" look and headed for his lounge room to watch television. I felt very intrusive and uncomfortable, but Phyllis re-assured me that this was normal for David, he was just a lovable "grump", and not to take any notice. Later that day when everyone was in a more relaxed mood and we were enjoying the jambalaya, I summoned up the courage to ask David what he had to say about his wife's jambalaya. His reply was, "Not a goddamn thing!", as he tucked into it with gusto. I explained that I would be writing his exact words in my book. He laughed, at last, "Go right on ahead", he said. David the grump had thawed, and we became friends. The reason why I am telling you all this is to let you know the power of a jambalaya when cooked as well as Phyllis's.

250 g/8 oz butter

2 medium onions, peeled and finely sliced

2 garlic cloves, peeled and finely sliced

2 teaspoons cayenne pepper

1 tablespoon paprika

1/2 teaspoon garlic powder

1 teaspoon salt

250 ml/8 fl oz cream of mushroom soup (home-made or canned)

1 litre/1 3/4 pints seafood stock (page 10) or chicken stock

250 g/8 oz each of: peeled prawns, peeled crawfish, and crabmeat

125 g/4 oz fresh parsley, finely chopped

125 g/4 oz spring onion tops, finely chopped

375 g/12 oz long-grain white rice

To serve:

Tabasco sauce (optional)

a fresh green salad

In a large cooking pot, melt the butter and sauté the onions, garlic and garlic powder for 4–5 minutes or until transparent. Stir in the cayenne pepper and paprika (they give the dish its colour), the garlic powder and salt. Cook for 2 minutes. Add the mushroom soup and stir over medium heat for another 3 minutes before you pour in the stock.

Allow the lot to simmer for about 5 minutes, then add just the prawns and crawfish, leaving the crabmeat until later. If it tears up too early, the crabmeat will look mushy and unattractive. Let the seafood cook for a minute before you stir in the parsley, spring onion tops and rice.

Taste the liquid and adjust the seasoning. Cover and simmer on low heat for 15 minutes, then stir in the crabmeat. Cover and cook on very low heat for 30–40 minutes or until all the liquid is absorbed and the rice is soft and cooked. Add a little more water if necessary. Serve hot, with some Tabasco sauce if you wish, and a fresh green salad.

Prawn Boulettes

SERVES 4–6 (10–12 pieces)

Instead of deep-frying the boulettes as instructed in this recipe, you can bake them in a pre-heated 180°C/350°F/Gas 4 oven for about 20–25 minutes.

1 kg/2 lb peeled cooked prawns, ground in a food processor

1 large onion, peeled and finely chopped

4 tablespoons fresh Cajun seasoning mix (page 9)

125 g/4 oz butter, melted

1 large egg, lightly beaten with a fork

salt and pepper to taste

500g/1lb dried breadcrumbs

vegetable oil for deep-frying

Mix together the prawns, onion and seasoning in a bowl. Cover and marinate in the refrigerator for 2–3 hours.

Remove from the refrigerator and add the remaining ingredients, except half the breadcrumbs and the oil. Mix thoroughly together.

Form the mixture into round balls, each one twice the size of your thumb (that's how my mum taught me to measure). Roll each boulette in the remaining breadcrumbs. Carefully arrange in a dish and return to the refrigerator for about 1 hour.

Before cooking, remove the boulettes from the refrigerator and let them stand at room temperature for at least 15 minutes.

Heat the oil in a non-stick skillet or frying pan and deep-fry the boulettes in small batches until cooked through and golden, about 3–4 minutes. Remove from the oil with a slotted spoon and drain on paper towels. Serve hot, with tomato sauce seasoned with 1 teaspoon dry Cajun seasoning (page 9), or your favourite dip.

Stuffed Mushrooms

CHAMPIGNONS BOURRIS

SERVES 4–6

Isn't it interesting how the mere aroma of some foods can trigger memories of places, events and festivals, however small? I had this dish on my first trip to Lafayette, Louisiana. It was a warm March evening and I had been working and flying around the United States. I arrived in Lafayette hot, sweaty and bothered, and a little peckish but not in the mood for a big meal. All I wanted was something light, tasty and quick, so my friends and I went to a local restaurant called Pat's Diner, and there I ate the most memorable mushrooms, exquisitely stuffed with seafood. It woke me up all right, and I have been making it ever since.

8 large mushrooms, stalks removed and reserved

60 g/2 oz finely grated Parmesan cheese

30 g/1 oz butter

For the stuffing:

2 mushrooms

90 g/3 oz butter

2 shallots, peeled and very finely chopped, or 2 spring onions complete with green tops, very finely chopped

2 garlic cloves, peeled and very finely chopped

1 teaspoon chopped fresh lemon-scented thyme

125 g/4 oz loose crabmeat, very finely chopped

2 teaspoons dry Cajun seasoning mix (page 9)

2 teaspoons fresh lemon juice

salt and pepper to taste

90 g/3 oz fine dried breadcrumbs

60 g/2 oz finely grated Parmesan cheese

90 ml/3 fl oz sweet sherry (optional)

Pre-heat the oven to 230°C/450°F/Gas 8.

First make the stuffing: chop the 2 mushrooms very finely with the reserved mushroom stalks from the large mushrooms. In a heavy-based skillet or frying pan, melt the butter and add the chopped mushrooms and stalks, the shallots, garlic and thyme. Sauté on medium heat, stirring all the time, until the vegetables are soft, about 5–10 minutes.

Add the crabmeat, seasoning mix and lemon juice and continue to cook for a further 3–5 minutes. Season to taste.

Finally, drain off any excess oil and stir in the breadcrumbs and Parmesan cheese. Mix well to blend and form a solid but soft stuffing. If the mixture turns out too dry, add a few tablespoons of sweet sherry to soften it.

Scoop spoonfuls of the stuffing into the inverted large mushroom cups and carefully stuff each cavity. Arrange the stuffed mushrooms in a non-stick or greased baking dish, sprinkle with the Parmesan and dot the top of each mushroom with a small piece of butter. Bake in the oven for about 15–20 minutes until they turn golden. Serve hot.

Cajun Seafood Salad

SERVES 4–6

This is a refreshing summer salad which leaves you wanting more, long after the last mouthful has disappeared. You can use any dressing you choose but, since it's a Cajun salad, I like to stick with a good vinaigrette with a dash of Cajun seasoning.

500 g/1 lb cooked large prawns

500 g/1 lb white crabmeat, shredded

1 tablespoon dry Cajun seasoning mix (page 9)

1 head of Iceberg lettuce, leaves separated

½ red cabbage, cored and sliced into thin strips

1 green and 1 red pepper (capsicums), de-seeded and sliced into thin strips

2 celery sticks, cut into thin half circles

8 oz/250 g chopped spring onion tops or chives

vinaigrette (see method)

4 large eggs, hard-boiled, shelled and cut into quarters

4 large ripe tomatoes, cut into quarters

juice of 1 lemon or 1 lime mixed with 1 teaspoon caster sugar

1 tablespoon chopped fresh parsley

De-vein the prawns: cut down the line of the spine with a sharp knife just deep enough to expose the vein without cutting right through the prawn. Remove and discard this vein, then wash the prawns and pat them dry.

Put the prawns and crabmeat in a bowl and sprinkle with the seasoning mix. Toss the seasoning through, cover and place in the refrigerator.

In a large salad bowl, combine the lettuce, cabbage, peppers, celery and spring onion tops or chives. Pour in the vinaigrette and toss through. Arrange the prawns, crabmeat, eggs and tomatoes on top of the salad greens, then sprinkle with the lemon juice mixture and the parsley. Serve with bread or Cornbread (page 31), or eat as is.

Vinaigrette

Put a pinch of salt into 60 ml/2 fl oz cider vinegar in a glass jar with a screw top, replace the lid and shake well to mix. Add 1 peeled and finely chopped garlic clove, 1 teaspoon Dijon mustard, 1 teaspoon lime or lemon juice, 125 ml/4 fl oz olive oil and ¼ teaspoon dry Cajun seasoning mix (page 9). Shake all together well and use as directed.

Hush Puppies

CORNBREAD FRITTERS

MAKES 24–30

When serving fish dishes, I guess it is fair to say that no Southern culinary expert would be seen dead without their hush puppies. Stories abound as to why or how the name came about, ranging from trying to silence dogs of the time by feeding them these fritters, to how contentedly and quietly people slept after eating them, like puppies in fact. Whatever the origins, the end result is finger-snapping good.

250 g/8 oz fine cornmeal (polenta)

125 g/4 oz self-raising flour

60 g/2 oz cornflour

3 teaspoons baking powder

2 teaspoons dry Cajun seasoning mix (page 9)

3 shallots, peeled and very finely chopped, or 3 spring onions, very finely chopped

2 garlic cloves, peeled and finely chopped

190 ml/6 fl oz milk or buttermilk

1 tablespoon butter

2 large eggs, lightly beaten with a fork

corn or other vegetable oil for deep-frying

Combine the cornmeal, flour, cornflour, baking powder, seasoning mix, shallots or spring onions and garlic in a large mixing bowl.

Heat the milk and butter together in a saucepan on medium heat until the butter has melted and the milk is warm. Make a well in the middle of the dry ingredients and stir in the beaten eggs followed by the milk and butter. Stir together to mix well.

In a heavy-based skillet or frying pan, heat up the oil until hot. Form the hush puppy mixture into tablespoonfuls and fry in small batches until cooked through and golden all over, about 3–4 minutes each. Remove from the oil and drain on paper towels. Serve hot, by themselves or with catfish or other dishes of choice.

Pain Perdu

SERVES 4–6

Pain perdu literally means "lost bread". The original descendant of this dish is a savoury French toast eaten at breakfast: stale bread dunked in beaten egg and milk, then fried to hide the staleness. In the Cajun version here, America meets France to deliver a dessert version of a classic French breakfast. The Cajuns have always been resourceful, they waste nothing, so they'd naturally preserve this brilliant tradition of giving stale bread a facelift.

4 eggs

500 ml/16 fl oz milk

125 g/4 oz caster sugar

1/2 teaspoon vanilla extract

125 g/4 oz butter

60 ml/2 fl oz vegetable oil

8 slices of stale bread

500 ml/16 fl oz maple syrup

2 level teaspoons freshly grated nutmeg

whipped fresh cream, to serve (optional)

Pre-heat the oven to 180°C/350°F/Gas 4.

First blend the eggs in a blender for 5 seconds, then add the milk, sugar and vanilla and blend again for about 15 seconds. Pour the mixture into a wide dish. In a small saucepan, melt together the butter and oil. Put a generous tablespoon of the oil mixture into a heavy-based skillet or frying pan and heat. When the oil is hot, soak each slice of bread in the egg and milk blend and fry on both sides until golden brown and cooked through, about 2–3 minutes each side. Remove from the heat, arrange in an ovenproof dish and keep warm in the oven until all the slices of bread are cooked. Pour maple syrup over each one and sprinkle with nutmeg. Serve hot, with whipped cream if you wish.

Bread Pudding with Rum Sauce

SERVES 4–6

This is one of those old English desserts that claims a different nationality every time it teams up with an exotic sauce. It is eaten almost everywhere the English have been. In the South of the United States of America, bread pudding has survived since the British left by draping itself alternately in whisky and rum sauce. It is now a delicious part of the cuisine, alternately Cajun and Southern.

10 thick slices of stale bread or half a stale baguette

375 ml/12 fl oz milk

125 ml/4 fl oz cream or canned evaporated milk

4 eggs

250 g/8 oz caster sugar

1 teaspoon freshly grated nutmeg

1 teaspoon vanilla extract

1 teaspoon ground cinnamon

125 g/4 oz ground pecans

250 g/8 oz raisins

90 g/3 oz butter

Rum Sauce (below), to serve

Rum Sauce

250 ml/8 fl oz milk

250 ml/8 fl oz canned evaporated milk

250 g/8 oz caster sugar

45 g/1 1/2 oz butter

2 teaspoons cornflour

90 ml/3 fl oz good-quality rum

Cut the bread into 5 cm/2 inch squares or cubes. Grease a medium-size casserole dish with butter. In a blender, combine the milk, cream, eggs, sugar, nutmeg, vanilla and cinnamon and blend well together.

Divide the bread, pecans and raisins into two parts. Arrange one half of the bread around the base of casserole, sprinkle with half the pecans and half the raisins, the pour half the milk mixture evenly over them. Repeat with the other half. Dot the top of the pudding with small portions of the butter.

Cover and allow to stand in a cool place for about 30 minutes to allow the milk custard to soak into the bread.

Pre-heat the oven to 180°C/350°F/Gas 4.

After 30 minutes, bake the pudding in the oven for about 1 hour until the pudding rises, the top is golden and the pudding is cooked through. Turn off the oven and allow the pudding to cool a little. Slice and serve hot, but not boiling hot, with Rum Sauce.

Rum Sauce

Combine the milks, sugar and butter in a saucepan and heat on low heat, stirring, until the sugar has dissolved and the mixture is hot. Blend the cornflour with 2 tablespoons lukewarm water and stir it into the hot milk mixture. Once thickened, remove from the heat and stir in the rum. Serve hot, over the bread pudding. You may prefer to use more rum, according to personal preference.

Spiced Coffee

SERVES 4-6

I guess I'm not surprised to find spiced coffee as part of the Cajun cuisine. Cajun is synonymous with spice, so why should the coffee be exempt? It is delicious, a neat way to finish a meal, and it leaves a lovely aromatic aftertaste.

6 rounded tablespoons freshly ground coffee

1.5 l/2¼ pints water

¾ teaspoon ground cinnamon

½ teaspoon freshly grated nutmeg

6–8 whole cloves

whipped cream (optional), to serve

Put the coffee in a large coffee pot and add the cinnamon, nutmeg and cloves. Brew as usual, with 1.5 litres/3 pints boiling water. Allow to stand and brew for at least 5–7 minutes, longer if you prefer strong coffee.

Strain and pour into coffee cups or coffee mugs. Top with whipped cream if you wish, or serve according to personal taste.

Green Cooler

SERVES 4–6

Make your own limeade or limefizz (below), or buy it ready-made.

750 ml/1¼ pints limeade or limefizz

375 ml/12 fl oz vodka

crushed ice

fresh lime slices, to garnish

Combine the limeade or limefizz in a blender and blend for about 5–10 seconds. Fill chilled glasses with crushed ice and pour the green cooler over the ice. Serve immediately, garnished with slices of lime.

Limeade/Limefizz

SERVES 4–6

Stir together 500 ml/16 fl oz lime cordial with 750 ml/1¼ pints chilled soda water or fizzy (sparkling) mineral water.

African American Tastes

Easter Day at the First African Baptist Church in Savannah, Georgia

Nearly everyone has heard of Southern cooking: Southern fried chicken, chicken Maryland, Carolina rice, Virginia hams, Southern fried oysters, she-crab soup, grits and chitterlings, peach cobbler and mint julep – all served up with the legendary "Southern hospitality".

It is a cuisine and a lifestyle which has evolved from a combination of some of the richest and poorest of tables and cooking pots. A blending of wealth and plenty with creativity and expertise dragged from another culture the other side of the globe.

Jamestown, in the Southern state of Virginia, was the first English colony in America. Settled in 1607, the small community struggled to survive – even with the help of the local Native Americans, who taught them how to cultivate beans, peas, pumpkins, squash and their staple foodstuff, maize (corn). Over the years, the mainly male settlers brought horses, pigs, cattle, goats, chickens and sheep from England. They import-

ed European cereals, such as wheat and barley, and they introduced apples and root vegetables.

Barely twelve years later, the colony imported its first batch of slaves from Africa, and the next century and a half saw the import of many more slaves.

The African population soon outnumbered the white colonists, making possible a highly labour intensive way of life in the rice fields and on cotton and tobacco plantations. Increasing prosperity allowed the building of grand homes, where a lavish style of life and hospitality burgeoned. To support such extravagance, the well-off continued to increase the slave population until, by the beginning of the Civil War in 1861, the majority of the four million slaves in the US were in the Southern states.

"The Gentry pretend to have their victuals drest, and serv'd up as Nicely as at the best Tables in London", the Virginia historian, Robert Beverley, drily noted in 1705. The South by then had its plantation society, its good life in the "syllabub era" of mint julep, elegant colonial houses and profuse hospitality with quantities of fresh, locally produced as well as imported foods, wines and spirits. But the fame of Southern cooking in those days rested entirely on the creative skills of the African cooks, who literally "slaved away" in vast, swelteringly hot kitchens with open hearths over which hung spits and cauldrons. If the cooks were amazed by the quantities of strange, foreign ingredients brought to the kitchen, it was not evident. They transformed the dull, traditional English fare into a unique and truly multi-cultural cuisine, using African seasonings and ingredients along with

Native American wild foods and exotic imports from Spain and France. African cooks brought their own cooking traditions and ingredients such as okra, black-eyed peas (beans), benne (sesame seeds), yams, peanut oil, joloff rice and coconut. They transformed the traditional English breads, cakes, trifles, syllabubs, "custardy egg and butter rich pastries" and pies, and ensured that the now legendary Southern sweet tooth had plenty of delicious varieties from which to choose.

But that is only half the story of Southern cooking. More recently, there has been a fashion for what is loosely described as "soul food". Soul food is a term used by African Americans to express something that is natural, open and sharing. It is simple, thrifty but wholesome home cooking, and is derived from the meals that African slaves were able to make from the poorest, most meagre foodstuffs supplied to the families of slaves. The African cook, so heartily praised in the plantation kitchens, brought all her talent and knowledge, developed from years of necessity, to cooking meals for herself and her family. She had to make do with whatever was available, including what could be raised or grown. Turnip tops, collard greens, beans and kale became the staples. The leftovers from pig carcasses were used in all sorts of imaginative ways, such as pork ribs, hocks, feet, ears, backbones and chitterlings (fried slices of small intestine). African cooks made full use of plentiful supplies of pig fat, frying everything – fish, meat and vegetables – until deliciously crisp, and serving it with herbs and spices, and hot, peppery sauces. Locally grown rice was plentiful, and is central to most soul food dishes, and corn, the great mainstay, was used to make cornbread, hominy and grits. Exhausted from long days in the fields or kitchens, women often felt revived in spirit as they cooked up some tasty food for their hungry families. Cooking was their way of nurturing and providing for their families, quite different from the ostentatious tables of the colonial gentry. Ruth Gaskins, a food his-torian from Virginia, recalled, "The only real comfort came at the end of the day, when we took either the food that we were given, or the food we raised, or the food we caught, and we put it in the pot, and we sat with our own kind and talked and sang and ate."

Dorinda writes:

"As I write this chapter I am re-visiting the early African American cooks, displaced and forced into subservience, with the fundamental human right of freedom of expression taken away on all fronts. I am thinking how necessity became the mother of their inventions in the kitchen. How in their struggle to express themselves, the kitchen and its contents became their culinary canvas, upon which they let their imaginations run free. This is my tribute to those courageous spirits, through whose ingenuity and ver-satility we can today enjoy these many delicious recipes. We owe it to them and many others, to carry forward the culinary torch.

Southern cooking is primarily a marriage between English, African and Native American – with Spanish, Italian, Jewish, German, Portuguese and others as wedding guests."

Ernestine the taxi driver invites me to dinner

Okra and Seafood Gumbo

SERVES 4–6

There are some ingredients which have become indelibly etched into the cooking pots of the history of food, not just black people's food, but good food, and I guess okra and seafood are such ingredients. Like them or not, they are here to stay in one form or another. Depending on the nationality and expertise of the cook, the combination can be transformed into meals for prince or peasant. A gumbo cooked with okra is referred to as gumbo févi.

500 g/1 lb peeled large prawns

100 ml/3½ fl oz corn or other vegetable oil

2 large onions, peeled and finely chopped

2 shallots, peeled and finely chopped, or 2 spring onions with green tops, chopped

3 garlic cloves, peeled and finely chopped

2 celery sticks with green tops, washed and very finely chopped

125 g/4 oz pepper (capsicum), de-seeded and finely diced

1 kg/2 lb okra, topped, tailed and sliced into thin rounds

3 tablespoons plain flour

1.5 litres/2½ pints shellfish stock

250 g/8 oz tomatoes, blanched and diced

3 tablespoons very finely chopped fresh parsley

salt and pepper to taste

1 teaspoon cayenne pepper (optional)

250 g/8 oz white crabmeat, broken into large pieces

De-vein the prawns: cut down the line of the spine with a sharp knife just deep enough to expose the vein without cutting right through the prawn. Remove and discard the vein, then wash the prawns and pat them dry. Sometimes you can buy pre-prepared prawns at your fishmonger, but naturally they cost a little more.

In a large cooking pot or heavy-based saucepan, heat up half the oil. Add the onions, shallots or spring onions, garlic, celery and pepper and sauté until soft and browning.

Add the okra and cook on medium heat until it is soft and limp, stirring all the time to prevent sticking. Remove from the heat, drain off any excess oil and put the vegetables in a heatproof dish. Set aside.

Clean the pan and heat up the remaining oil in it until hot. Add the flour and stir briskly with a wire whisk to make a brown roux.

Carefully stir in small amounts of the shellfish stock until all is used up. Add the tomatoes and sautéed vegetables, the parsley and salt and pepper. If you like hot food, add the cayenne. Simmer for about 15 minutes, then add the prawns and crabmeat. Simmer until everything is well cooked and the stock has reduced and thickened a little. Serve hot, spooned over boiled, long-grain rice, or serve the gumbo and rice separately.

Southern Fried Chicken

SERVES 4–6

This famous dish remains as tasty as ever, even in today's health-conscious society. I guess there are ways around everything if you really try. Some people use just seasonings and flour, some use eggs or milk as the binder – and some others have adulterated the time-honoured taste of this chicken to such an extent that it no longer bears any resemblance to the taste of old. My belief is that if you want the true taste of something, then don't compromise. Eat it as it is meant to be eaten and get out there and exercise, if you really must. Here it is then, without compromise, the finger-licking, lip-smacking, Southern fried chicken of old.

1–1.5 kg/2–3 lb chicken, cut into 8–10 portions, or 12 chicken drumsticks or legs

salt and lots of freshly ground black pepper

6 teaspoons paprika

6 teaspoons celery salt

6 teaspoons onion powder

3 teaspoons mustard powder

1 teaspoon cayenne pepper

3 large eggs

1 kg/2 lb plain flour

oil for frying

Clean the chicken and pat it dry with paper towels. Place it in a large bowl.

Mix together the salt, black pepper, paprika, celery salt, onion powder, mustard powder and cayenne pepper. Divide into three equal portions and sprinkle one portion over the chicken pieces. Toss the pieces together so that each piece gets coated with some seasoning. You may prefer to put all the chicken pieces in a clear plastic bag instead of in a bowl, sprinkle with the seasoning, then seal and shake to coat.

Cover and leave to stand for 45 minutes to 1 hour.

Beat the eggs in a bowl until light and fluffy. Add one-third of the seasoning and beat to combine. Mix the remaining third of the seasoning with the flour.

Heat up the oil in a deep heavy-based skillet or frying pan. Dip each piece of chicken into the egg, then dredge it in the seasoned flour. Fry the chicken in batches in the hot oil for about 6–8 minutes until each piece is well cooked and golden. Make sure the chicken does not brown too quickly on the outside and remain uncooked on the inside. To see if the chicken is properly cooked, prick the pieces with a skewer: if clear liquid comes out, this is the sign that it is cooked on the inside as well as the outside. Keep warm in oven while cooking the remainder of the chicken. Serve hot, with rice or potatoes and a green salad.

The Ultimate Macaroni Cheese

SERVES 4–6

Macaroni cheese is very popular with African Americans. Quite apart from the obvious economic reasons, I cannot exactly trace how this came to be such a strong part of present-day African American cooking. I can only surmise that this, like other pasta and ice cream, is part of the Italian influence on American food. I had to include it because it's on just about every menu in the South. Besides, it's delicious.

salt

250 g/8 oz macaroni

125 g/4 oz butter

2 spring onions/scallions, finely sliced into rounds

2 tablespoons plain flour

250 ml/8 fl oz canned evaporated milk

250 ml/8fl oz single cream

2 tablespoons mayonnaise

310 g/10 oz sharp mature Cheddar cheese, grated

salt and pepper to taste

1–2 eggs, lightly beaten with a fork (optional)

125 g/4 oz Parmesan cheese, freshly grated or ready-grated from a drum

Fill a large saucepan with water, add 1 teaspoon of salt and bring it to a boil. Carefully pour the macaroni into the boiling water and cook for about 10 minutes until the texture is al dente (tender but firm to the bite). Do not overcook the macaroni or it will get mushy when cooked again in the oven. Remove from the heat, drain and set aside.

Pre-heat the oven to 180°C/350°F/Gas 4. Grease a 2 litre/4 pint casserole dish.

In a heavy-based skillet or frying pan, melt the butter and sauté the spring onions on medium heat until soft (about 3–4 minutes). Add the flour and stir to mix well. Continue to sauté for about 3 minutes, then blend in first the evaporated milk, then the cream, and then the mayonnaise. Finally, blend in the grated Cheddar cheese. Season to taste.

If you like an even richer macaroni cheese, stir 1–2 beaten eggs through the macaroni until evenly combined.

Mix the macaroni with the cheese sauce and pour into the greased casserole. Sprinkle the top liberally with the grated Parmesan cheese and bake in the oven for about 20–30 minutes or until the top has browned and macaroni is piping hot. Turn off the heat and allow the macaroni cheese to cool down in the oven – it tastes best when allowed to cool down a little. Serve warm to hot, with a fresh salad.

A Change of Heart
I must admit I was very disappointed the first time I was served macaroni cheese for dinner in the USA. It was Hallowe'en, kids were busy "trick-or-treating", and a friend in Los Angeles invited me to visit her. Our hostess was terribly excited about her macaroni cheese, which we were about to devour. Having eaten masses of macaroni cheese in England, I could not share her enthusiasm. I regarded it as a boring and bland comfort food. My opinion did not change that day, but it did when I tasted macaroni cheese again in Savannah. I did a double-flip, and asked for the recipe.

One Pot Pork

SERVES 4–6

Notwithstanding certain current religious practices, the love of pork and one pot cooking is very West African even to this day! It has become a part of the African legacy in the south and not just for African Americans, it is also very common in Cajun cooking practice. The style first arrived in the Caribbean with the African slaves, eventually ending up around Charleston and Savannah, and later spread to other parts of America. In this recipe, the dish is no longer plain. It has become Americanized.

2 large sweet potatoes

1 large aubergine

30 ml/1 fl oz vegetable oil

2 tablespoons cornflour

3 teaspoons garlic salt

3 teaspoons paprika

8 lean pork chops, with little or no fat

60 ml/2 fl oz hot water

1 large red onion, peeled and sliced into thin rings

8 large, ripe tomatoes, blanched, peeled and pulped, or 500 g/1 lb can chopped tomatoes

250 ml/8 fl oz Moselle or semi-sweet fruity white wine

1 large cooking apple

2 teaspoons brown sugar

leaves from 1 bunch of fresh basil

1 tablespoon chopped fresh oregano

salt and pepper to taste

Peel the sweet potatoes and aubergine and cut them into thin rounds. Heat up the oil in a heavy-based skillet or frying pan and quickly brown the sweet potato and aubergine rounds in small batches without overcooking. Remove from the oil and set aside.

Mix the cornflour, garlic salt and paprika together. Dredge each pork chop through this spiced mixture to coat all sides, then fry in the hot oil until lightly browned on the outside. Drain off any excess oil. Transfer the pork to large heavy-based cooking pot or saucepan.

De-glaze the skillet or frying pan with the hot water and pour this over the chops.

Arrange the onion rings on top of the chops and add the tomatoes. Mix the remaining spiced cornflour mixture with the wine and add this too. Simmer slowly on low heat.

Peel and core the apple, slice it into thin rounds and arrange on top of the pork as well. Sprinkle with the sugar, whole basil leaves, chopped oregano and seasoning to taste. Partially cover the pan and continue to simmer for about 20–30 minutes until the chops and vegetables are tender and the sauce has thickened. Serve hot, with boiled rice or Hoppin' John (page 34).

Candied Yams

SERVES 3–4

This dish is made with sweet potatoes, not the real yams as we know them in Africa – the rough and brown-skinned, fat, sometimes hairy, tuberous and starchy root vegetables. The vegetables used in this dish are definitely sweet potatoes – they're smooth, with a colourful variety of orange, purple or white skins, and are much sweeter than yams when cooked. And so the confusion reigns over sweet potatoes versus yams. Should they be called yams or sweet potatoes? As long as you and I know which we use how and when, we'll be fine.

3 large sweet potatoes

90 g/3 oz sugar

60 g/2 oz butter

3 tablespoons fresh lemon juice

3 tablespoons dark rum

¹/₂ teaspoon ground cinnamon

¹/₂ teaspoon peeled and grated fresh root ginger

Pre-heat the oven to 200°C/400°F/Gas 6.

Prick all over the sweet potatoes with a fork. Bake them in their skins for about 20–30 minutes until cooked. Do not overcook. They need to be soft but firm, not squashy. Remove from the oven, allow to cool, then peel off and discard the skin. Cut the potatoes into thick rounds and arrange in a greased casserole dish.

In a non-stick saucepan, combine the sugar, butter, lemon juice, rum, cinnamon and ginger. Boil on medium heat, stirring all the time, until reduced to a syrup. Pour the syrup all over the sweet potatoes and return to the oven. Bake for 15–20 minutes or until the top is brown. Serve hot.

You Say Potato . . .

Sweet potatoes and yams are both delicious and popular staple root vegetables. Their above-ground foliage and antics are similar, but there the similarity ends and the confusion begins. The reality is, they are not of the same botanical family. The sweet potato is known as *ipomeo batatas* and belongs to the *convolvulaceae* family of plants, while the yam goes by *dioscorea batatas* and belongs to the *dioscoreaceae* group of plants. The sweet potato is the better known and more versatile of the two vegetables, hence it is more popular with other cultures. A great many years ago somebody got the names confused, so I'm afraid we are now stuck with yams for sweet potatoes as well as for yams themselves.

Spoon Bread

SERVES 4–6

This is comfort food at its gourmet best, and the only thing I can say about it is to warn unwary newcomers. Spoon bread is addictive. It is so easy to make and yet so difficult to get out of your mind. It is simply divine. Some people call it batter bread, but the name spoon bread I suspect refers to how it is served. You spoon it out of the baking dish on to your plate rather like one would do with mashed potato or ice cream. There are many ways to make spoon bread, so you can devise your own using different vegetables with the basic binders of eggs, cornmeal, milk, baking powder, water and seasoning.

500 ml/16 fl oz water

1/2 teaspoon salt

250 g/8 oz white or yellow cornmeal (polenta)

250 ml/8 fl oz low-fat milk

30 g/1 oz butter, melted

1 teaspoon baking powder

1/4 teaspoon cayenne pepper

2 garlic cloves, peeled and finely chopped

1 onion, peeled and very finely chopped

1/4 teaspoon black pepper

3 egg yolks (optional)

250 g/8 oz Cheddar cheese, grated

3 egg whites

1 tablespoon caster sugar

6 large spinach leaves, cleaned and dried, then rolled tightly and sliced into very fine strips

Pre-heat the oven to 190°C/350°F/Gas 4. Grease a 3 litre/6 pint casserole dish.

Bring the water and salt to a boil in a large saucepan. Add the cornmeal, lower the heat and cook for about 1–2 minutes, stirring all the time. Remove from the heat and stir in the milk, butter, baking powder, cayenne, garlic, onion, black pepper, egg yolks (if using) and cheese. Cover and set aside.

In a large mixing bowl, beat the egg whites until light peaks form, add the sugar and continue beating until solid peaks form. First fold in the cornmeal mixture and then the spinach. Pour into the greased casserole. Bake, uncovered, in the oven for about 45 minutes to 1 hour until set. Serve hot or cold, it's just as delicious either way.

Dorinda's Sweet Cornbread

SERVES 4–6

The favourite of young and old, cornbread can be served sweet or savoury. In most Southern households, meals are not complete unless served with cornbread. America, courtesy of the Native Americans, has taken cornmeals to her palate, and every cook has their own recipe, complete with variations. Here is one of mine for a light and floaty sweet cornbread.

250 g/8 oz fine white or yellow corn-meal (polenta)

125 g/4 oz self-raising flour

125 g/4 oz cornflour

180 g/6 oz caster sugar

1 rounded teaspoon baking powder

90 g/3 oz butter

375 ml/12 fl oz milk

2 large eggs, lightly beaten with a fork

a pinch of salt

Pre-heat the oven to 180°C/350°F/Gas 4 and place a 30 x 20 cm/13 x 9 inch baking tray in the oven to warm up while making preparations.

Put the cornmeal in a large mixing bowl and mix in the self-raising flour, cornflour, sugar and baking powder.

Melt most of the butter in a saucepan, leaving 1 tablespoon aside for later. Add the milk to the melted butter and warm up on medium heat. Do not boil. When warm, stir in the lightly beaten eggs and the salt. Remove the mixture from the heat.

Make a well in the middle of the flour mixture and pour in the milk and butter mixture. Blend by hand with a wooden spoon. Remove the heated baking tray from the oven and grease with some butter or corn oil. Pour the mixture into the tray. Bake, uncovered, in the oven for 20–25 minutes until the bread is firm and springs back when pressed. Remove from the oven.

Melt the remaining butter and brush the top of the cornbread with it. Allow the cornbread to stand for 5 minutes before cutting into slices. Serve warm or cool, as you wish.

Cornbread à la Ernestine

SERVES 4–6

I have been making different types of cornbread for years, but now here I was at last in Savannah, Georgia, "The South" of the United States, home of cornbread, discussing cornbread with a local taxi driver called Ernestine. You know, we have a saying in Ghana, my country of origin, "travel and see". I did, and in true Southern style, Ernestine's hospitality didn't just stop at giving me her cornbread recipe, she invited me home to taste it. Hers is a savoury one.

500 g/1 lb fine white or yellow corn-meal (polenta)

250 g/8 oz plain flour

3 large eggs

125 g/4 oz butter

2 teaspoons salt

375 ml/12 fl oz milk

125 ml/4 fl oz water

1 teaspoon baking powder

Pre-heat the oven to 220°C/425°F/Gas 7. Grease a 25 cm/10 inch baking tin.

Put all the ingredients together in a large bowl and stir into a creamy mix. Pour into the greased tin.

Bake in the middle of the oven for 15–20 minutes or until cooked and firm. Serve hot, with anything of your choice, or with Collard Greens and Smoked Neck Bones (page 33) as Ernestine did.

Cornsticks

For corn sticks, use either of the cornbread recipe mixes, but bake in greased, cast-iron corn stick moulds. Cook for a shorter time (10-15 minutes), because the individual corn moulds are smaller and therefore cook quicker and burn quicker. Vary your flavours by adding bacon pieces with the fat already rendered, bits of finely chopped greens, or bits of dried fruit soaked in the recipe/cooking water for about 1 hour before using.

Opposite: Crawfish Boil (p.13); Following pages: Chicken and Andouille Sausage Gumbo (p.11); Sweet Potato and Pecan Pie (p.36).

Collard Greens and Smoked Neck Bones

SERVES 4–6

The quintessential "poor black" fare from the South, yet these days admission to liking it and a reference to it is no longer shameful. Well times may be changing, but for my money, tasty food will never have a race, colour nor social status. In short, good food by any other name is still good food, there to be enjoyed . And that is precisely what Ernestine and I did at her house in Savannah with her mother, the Reverend Owen and her twin sister Ethel.

2 litres/4 pints water

500 g/1 lb smoked neck bones or bacon bones

2 big bunches of collard greens, Swiss chard, silverbeet, mustard greens or kale

125 g/4 oz chopped bacon pieces

salt and pepper to taste

30 ml/1 fl oz corn oil or melted bacon dripping (optional)

1 tablespoon pepper sauce, or 1–2 red chillies, de-seeded and finely chopped (optional)

In a large saucepan, bring the water and neck bones to a boil. Lower the heat to medium and cook for about 45 minutes (1 1/4–1 1/2 hours if using Swiss chard or silverbeet later on in this recipe). Skim off and discard any froth or sediment that collects on top of the water. Remove the neck bones with a slotted spoon and set aside. Keep the water.

Clean up the greens, cut and discard the central stalks, then cut or tear the green leaves into strips. Put these in the same boiling water used for the neck bones and continue boiling for another 30 minutes. (If using Swiss chard, put it in with the neck bones at this stage.) Return the neck bones to the pan with the greens. Add the bacon pieces, pepper and oil or dripping (if using) and boil for another 30 minutes (5 minutes only for Swiss chard and silverbeet). Collard greens and neck bones take ages to soften. However, if you are using Swiss chard or silverbeet, the cooking time is of course much shorter for the greens. Remove from heat and drain off excess water when the neck bones and greens are cooked. Serve hot, with Hoppin' John (page 34) and Cornbread (page 32).

Illustrated opposite

Hoppin' John

SERVES 4–6

Hoppin' John is combined black-eyed peas (beans) and rice, a meal traditionally eaten by African Americans on New Year's Day to bring good luck for the rest of the year. There are different explanations for how the name came about, but my favourite one, even if it may not be the most authentic explanation, is the image of lots of little kids, loosely referred to as "Johns", hoppin' from one foot to the other around the dinner table in anticipation of second helpings of this perennial favourite. Just about all black cultures around the globe have this dish in one form or another.

250 g/8 oz black-eyed peas (beans)

750 ml/1¼ pints water

salt

500 g/1 lb long-grain rice

1 heaped teaspoon bicarbonate of soda

2 teaspoons brown sugar

1 tablespoon butter

2 tablespoons chopped fresh parsley

Rice

In the olden days, West African slaves were particularly popular in South Carolina because of their skills in cooking rice. They cooked it so that the grains separated individually. A skill still much prized among black people to this day. Until recently, Hoppin' John was regarded with a lot of snobbishness as food for the "poh blacks", but with the advent of beans as a health food, fashionable eateries are now serving it. Some other names for Hoppin' John are Rice and Peas (Caribbean), Black-eyed Beans and Rice, Whippoorwill Peas and Rice, and Crowder Peas and Rice (American South).

Damon Fowler told me Charlestonians are often compared to the Chinese because of their mutual love of rice, but Charlestonians would say the emphasis should actually be on how they differ from the Chinese, because the Chinese live on rice and worship their ancestors whereas the Charlestonians worship rice and live on their ancestors . . .

Put the peas (beans) in a large bowl and fill with lots of cold water to completely cover and drown the peas. Leave overnight to allow the peas to absorb water and expand.

The next day, rinse the peas thoroughly under the cold tap, place them in a large cooking pot with the measured water and some salt and bring to a boil. Add the bicarbonate of soda and sugar and cook for about 25–30 minutes hours until the peas are soft. Remove the pot from the heat and drain off the cooking water into a heavy-based cooking pot. Set the peas (beans) aside.

Add the rice to the cooking water, taste and season accordingly. Bring to a boil, lower the heat and cook on low until all the water is absorbed and the rice is cooked and soft, about 25–30 minutes. You may need to add about another 250 ml/8 fl oz water if the rice is still hard, to help it cook and soften. When the rice is cooked, combine the peas and rice in a large serving dish and stir in a knob of butter (about 1 tablespoon). Garnish with the parsley and eat by itself, or serve with anything you choose, it's good enough.

For the oven version: soak the peas overnight as before. Next day, rinse them thoroughly under the cold tap.

Pre-heat the oven to 220°C/425°F/Gas 7. Grease a 25 cm/10 inch baking tin.

Put the beans, water, rice, bicarbonate of soda, brown sugar, butter and a pinch of salt into a large bowl and stir together. Pour into the greased tin.

Bake in the middle of the oven for 45–60 minutes or until cooked and firm. Serve hot, with anything of your choice, or with Collard Greens and Smoked Neck Bones (page 33) as Ernestine did.

Peach Cobbler

SERVES 4–6

A cobbler is basically a deep fruit pie with some sort of crumble or pastry on top. It is one of the many legacies the English left behind in the South, where the commonest fruits for a cobbler are peaches and berries. My most memorable cobbler was at Nita's, a little "home away from home" restaurant with a constantly revolving clientele.

4 large ripe peaches, peeled and thickly sliced, with stones removed

180 ml/6 fl oz maple syrup

1 teaspoon ground nutmeg

1 teaspoon ground cinnamon

1/2 teaspoon ground cloves

1/4 teaspoon ground ginger

250 g/8 oz plain flour

250 ml/8 fl oz milk

2 large egg whites

180 ml/6 fl oz fresh cream, to serve

Pre-heat the oven to 190°C/375°F/Gas 5.

Arrange the peaches in a glass or presentable baking dish measuring about 20 cm/8 inches in diameter. Mix together the maple syrup with half the ground nutmeg, cinnamon, cloves and ginger. Drizzle this mixture over the peaches, making sure each piece of fruit is well coated. Allow to stand for 10–15 minutes.

In a mixing bowl, combine the flour, milk and egg whites and blend to mix. Pour carefully all over the top of the fruit. For a finale, sprinkle the other half of the spices all over the topping.

Bake, uncovered, in the middle of the oven for 45–50 minutes until the topping is cooked and beautifully browned. Serve hot or cooled down to room temperature, with fresh cream. Some people prefer their cobblers chilled. Well, serve as you wish.

Southern Desserts

In the olden days on the Southern plantations, the kitchens inside the main buildings got so intolerably hot that they had to be re-located outside, and of course the lady of the house left all the cooking to her cook, who was often black. She left all the cooking that is, except the sweets and desserts. She would start these herself and then pass them over to her cook to be finished off. The smart cooks would add a touch of this and a touch of that flavouring to enhance the dish. That is how we still have English desserts, but often with New World additions.

Sweet Potato and Pecan Pie

SERVES 6–8

Two Southern favourites come together in a delicious union. Each mouthful of this pie is to be savoured. Damon Fowler and I had fun cooking this in his Savannah kitchen. We agreed that this is one of the many Southern dishes which successfully marries the cultures that have helped shape its cuisine – Native American sweet potatoes and pecans, English pudding ways and African cooking skills.

shortcrust pastry (below), rolled into a 22.5 cm/9 inch square sheet

750 g/1 1/2 lb large sweet potatoes, roasted in their skins

125 g/4 oz brown or demerara sugar

2 large eggs, lightly beaten with a fork

1 tablespoon grated orange or lemon zest

1/2 teaspoon freshly grated nutmeg

2 tablespoons bourbon or cognac

a pinch of salt

60 ml/2 fl oz single cream

For the pecan topping:

125 g/4 oz caster sugar

1 egg white

2 teaspoons butter, melted

2–3 drops of vanilla extract

250 g/8 oz pecans

Pre-heat the oven to 230°C/450°F/Gas 8.

Grease a deep 20 cm/8 inch round pie dish and line it with short-crust pastry. Carefully push the pastry down to fit inside the dish, then trim off any excess around the edge with a knife. Press the prongs of a fork down on the pastry all round the top lip, to form a pattern and seal the pastry down.

Line the pastry with greaseproof paper, trimmed to fit. Fill the cavity with uncooked dry rice or beans as weights to keep the pastry down, then bake the pastry blind in the oven for about 7–8 minutes. It only needs to be part-cooked at this stage. Remove from the oven, remove the paper and rice or beans and let the pastry stand and cool as you prepare the filling. Turn the oven down to 180°C/350°F/Gas 4 and leave it on.

Peel the sweet potatoes and push them through a potato masher or sieve into a large bowl. Blend with a fork and add the brown sugar, then the lightly beaten eggs. Stir in the citrus zest and nutmeg. Add the bourbon or cognac and finally a tiny pinch of salt and the cream. Stir everything thoroughly to mix. Pour into the pastry case and set aside as you prepare the topping.

In a medium bowl, lightly whisk together the caster sugar, egg white, melted butter and vanilla extract for a few seconds until white but not fluffy. Stir in the pecans until well coated. Carefully pour the pecan mixture over the top of the sweet potato pie mix.

Taking care not to disturb the surface too much, carefully arrange the pecans in an attractive pattern on the top. Alternatively, you may find it easier to arrange the pecans attractively on top of the pie before you whisk together the sugar, egg white and vanilla, then carefully spread the egg white mixture well over the pecans.

Bake in the oven for 35 minutes until golden brown and set. Remove from the oven and rest the pie until cool. Serve at room temperature, with fresh cream or by itself.

Pastry

250 g/8 oz plain flour

2 tablespoons sugar

a pinch of salt

60 g/2 oz finely ground pecans (optional)

90 g/3 oz butter

I egg

up to 2 tablespoons milk

In a mixing bowl, first mix together the flour, sugar, salt and ground pecans (if using), then blend in the butter. Whisk the egg and milk separately in another bowl, then combine the two mixtures until a pastry dough is formed. If necessary, add 1/2 tablespoon more flour. Knead the dough together well, then form into a ball in the bowl. Cover and refrigerate for 30 minutes before using. This makes it slightly firmer and easier to work with. When ready, flour a board and a rolling pin, roll out the pastry to the required size and use according to your recipe.

Corinthian Mint Julep

SERVES 2

I suppose you couldn't really eat all that rich Southern food without something equally stunning and Southern to wash it down with, so here is a julep. I must confess that I chose this particular julep recipe not just for its fame as the drink of the South, but because it also has my middle name in it. It belongs to my friend Damon Fowler and I quote, "Corinthian in this case is a reference to St. Paul's Epistle to the Corinthians, chapter 13. The name is applied to a julep made with three jiggers of whisky – one each for faith, hope and charity." Now I have it on religious authority to drink the stuff, cheers!

6 jiggers (about 250 ml/8 fl oz) bourbon

4 large sprigs of fresh mint, each at least 5 cm/2 inches long

2 teaspoons sugar

4 tablespoons cold water

lots of crushed or shaved ice

Juleps

Juleps originated in Kentucky, the birth-place of bourbon. They were originally concocted to disguise the taste of poor-quality whisky, but of course nowadays whisky has better ingredients. This modern version of sweetened whisky, mint and crushed ice dates back to the mid to late 19th century. Believed to be the oldest recipe for julep, it is said to have come from Lettice Bryan's "The Kentucky Housewife".

If you have time – and forethought – it helps to chill the bottle of bourbon in the freezer for 24 hours before using. It won't freeze because of the alcohol, but it will cool down considerably and make the bourbon sluggish. This will help serve the julep at the right temperature – chilled.

Strip the leaves from two of the sprigs of mint, divide into two portions and place each half, together with equal parts of the sugar, at the bottom of two chilled (julep) tumblers. Add 2 tablespoons water to each tumbler and, using a long spoon, gently crush the mint leaves well into the sugar.

Pour in small amounts of the bourbon and stir well to dissolve most, if not all, of the sugar. Top with lots of ice and pour in the remaining bourbon. Stir the contents of the tumblers together without touching the tumblers until all of the outsides turn frosty. Garnish with the remaining mint and serve immediately.

Iced Tea

MAKES 2 LITRES/4 PINTS

This is a very popular drink throughout the United States, but perhaps more so in the warmer climates like the Southern belt because it is so refreshing when chilled. It also has the added bonus of being non-alcoholic and inexpensive. It has to be made well, not too sweet and not too bitter, and is best made with soft water that contains no chemicals or trace elements. If necessary, use bottled water. For authenticity and taste, it is best to use tea grown near Charleston by the American Classic Tea Company – if at all possible.

2 litres/4 pints clean cold water

125 g/4 oz black tea leaves (good-quality tea)

sugar to taste

4 small sprigs of fresh mint (optional)

lemon slices (optional), to serve

Pre-heat a large teapot with boiling water from a kettle filled from a household hot water tap. Let stand for 5–10 minutes.

Empty the kettle, re-fill with half the measured water from the recipe and bring to a boil. The water should be used immediately after it has boiled. Do not allow it to overboil, because this could cause clouding of the brew after refrigeration.

Empty and discard the boiling water from the now warmed teapot. Once empty, pour in the tea leaves and top with the freshly boiled water. Stir well to mix, then leave the tea to brew for about 5 minutes.

Strain the brew through a fine sieve to remove the tea leaves.

Pour the strained tea together with the remaining measured cold water into a large 2 litre/4 pint drinks jug. Add sugar to sweeten according to your individual taste and stir until it has dissolved. I find that the less sugar used the more refreshing the final drink. Add the mint leaves (if using) and chill the tea in the refrigerator until cold. Serve in glasses, with lemon slices if you like.

Chinese American Tastes

Shopping in Chinatown, San Francisco

In China, California is known as *Gum San*, meaning Gold Mountain, and San Francisco is called *Gum San Dai Fow* – Big City of the Gold Mountain.

Gold has always been a powerful magnet to men. The Chinese were no exception. The Great Gold Rush in California, which began around 1840, attracted miners and dreamers from many parts of the Old and New World; even as far afield as China. In particular, they came from the Gwandong Province, the capital of which was then called Canton, the name of the most popular of the many regional Chinese cuisines eaten in the West.

It has often been said that visitors from China had been to the Americas thousands of years before the gold rush. There are many stories, some probably true, but sadly there is little evidence to support them. Other gold strikes, such as the Yukon near Seattle, attracted numerous Chinese workers, and there were various other "golden" opportunities for

work, such as labouring on the construction of the Central Pacific Railroad. They were expected to feed themselves, which at least meant that their traditional diet of vegetables and rice was considerably healthier than that of other labourers. They boiled water for their Chinese tea and thus protected themselves from the often polluted water. Some found work as butchers, launderers and cooks for the huge gangs of labourers, miners and other new settlers. They set up as greengrocers and cultivated vegetable gardens to supply fresh produce, which they sold in baskets around town. They grew onions, oriental greens such as bok choy, lotus roots, gai lan, daikon and chrysanthemum leaves. Fish, especially salmon and rockfish, was once plentiful in the rich seas off the northwest coast. The Chinese became expert at preparing and canning fish so thay were employed in the canneries in large numbers.

Both Seattle in the northwest and San Francisco in the southwest have claims to be the "Gateway to Asia". However, the first restaurant called "The Canton" opened in San Francisco as early as 1849 and a thriving Chinatown community was already developing despite the many fires and earthquakes that nearly destroyed the city. Few Chinese, in the early years, regarded themselves as settlers or immigrants. Most came with the aim of sending money to their families living in extreme poverty back home in China. They hoped to save enough to return to China, buy land or set up in business. To Westerners,

Exotic foods like dried octopus can be found

Francisco had its own well-established and vibrant Chinatown filled with restaurants, shops and markets selling every variety of fresh and specially imported produce. Stalls, shop fronts, Chinese bakeries and delicatessens overflowed with delicious and fascinating-looking specialities: locally produced tofu and soya, Chinese sausage, dried noodles, duck and chicken feet, braised pig intestines and octopus, gingko nuts, lotus and bamboo leaves, water chestnuts and dried mushrooms, to name just a small selection.

At first, restaurants served Westernized Chinese dishes, creations for the American palate, such as sweet and sour dishes and chow mein, but as people began to appreciate the subtleties and flavours of Chinese cuisines, the restaurants flourished and a new enthusiasm emerged for authentic, even regional, specialities such as Szechuan, Hunan, Mandarin and Fukien. Chinese cookery books, such as *The Pleasure of Chinese Cooking* by Grace Chu, and Helen Brown's *The West Coast Cook Book*, became very popular, as Americans discovered the joys of eating out and cooking at home with Chinese ingredients and Chinese cooking methods using woks, bamboo

Chinese ways seemed very foreign. The Chinese kept to themselves and ate exotic foods such as raw fish and barely cooked strange vegetables, and they used herbal remedies. Despite the fact that many were employed as cooks and domestics, the Chinese were thought of as alien and dirty, partly because they scavenged the streets and garbage dumps to feed their pigs. However, Chinese food was probably far cleaner and healthier than other local fare. In fact the Chinese treated their food with the same sort of respect as did the Native Americans, who thought the Chinese were just another tribe and left them alone.

This hostility and intolerance culminated in the Chinese Exclusions Act in 1882, which made the Chinese the only ethnic group ever to be specifically barred from entering the USA. The Port Townsend Immigration Aid Society stated in 1889, "No person of American or European birth can begin to compete with these leprous creatures, because they cannot, will not and ought not to live as they do". Because of this, the numbers of Chinese in America was halved over the next twenty years.

Despite these harsh and inhuman conditions, the Chinese and people from other parts of Asia found ways to continue entering and working in America. Gradually attitudes changed, and by the 1950s San

Andy, the master chef, in his 'Harborside' restaurant in San Francisco

steamers and chopsticks. The Chinese, like the Italians, are naturals in the restaurant trade because celebrating and sharing food is fundamental to their culture.

Famine and poverty have plagued Chinese history and they have come to value the pleasures of simple and healthy food. In many parts of China, firewood was in short supply and foodstuffs such as meat were scarce. Every scrap of food had to be used and cooked quickly. Their method was to chop everything small and fry it fast, popularly known as "stir-fry". The combinations were endless, and their ingenuity in creating a tasty and nutritious meal with numerous small dishes seasoned with herbs, spices and Chinese sauces gave rise to the term *tsap sui*, or as the Americans came to call it, chop suey. *Tsap sui* is Cantonese for "miscellaneous things" or "fried miscellaneous", to be eaten with the staples of rice or noodles.

Another hugely popular meal is *dim sum*, which means "point to the heart". Its attraction to Americans is, like *tsap sui* and other Chinese specialities, a table of many different dishes which everyone can share together. *Dim sum* is served from carts or trolleys, there is no menu, you just dive in and try your luck! Eating Chinese is always a culinary adventure as well as a lively social occasion, and that is part of its attraction.

Chinese Americans are enthusiastic about their new identity and culture, but they have also guarded their traditions and honoured their cultural roots. Respect for family, ancestors and spiritual values are inherent in Chinese American homes today. Symbolism is also still important in Chinese American culture. For example, colours carry great significance. Red is the colour for happiness and vitality, green represents life and abundance, blue is the colour of heaven and tranquillity, and yellow or gold is for wealth, property and power. Many foods also have a symbolic meaning. No wonder Chinese dishes look so colourful and appetizing.

For the gourmet who loves all kinds of Asian food, Chinatown in San Francisco is a perfect heaven. It also boasts huge numbers of restaurants serving not only a wide range of Chinese regional specialities, but also Japanese, Thai, Vietnamese, Korean, Filipino, Malay and many other equally fascinating and delicious cuisines.

Dorinda writes:
"What I have grown to love about Chinese and other Asian food is the wholeness of the meals – the way in which they are not just concerned to provide delicious fuel for the body, but also to cater for the mind and soul as well. The concept of 'you are what you eat' has long been well understood by the Chinese. They have always been acutely aware of the need to balance the Yin and Yang in life, and food is a part of that life."

Note: The savoury recipes given in this chapter are meant to be served as part of a meal comprising several dishes. If you want to eat them as a main course on their own, increase the quantities accordingly.

Dorina doing Tai Chi in Jackson Square, San Francisco

Sizzling Rice Soup

SERVES 4–6

This soup takes a while to prepare, so allow plenty of time. It also makes good use of that part of the rice that most households usually discard as useless when they burn their steamed rice. Yes, I'm referring to the crust or burnt bit at the bottom of the pot. It is interesting to note that in parts of West Africa, this part of the rice is actually regarded as a delicacy, and kids have been known to jostle over who is going to get it first! From now on, save yours in the freezer until needed for a delicious soup like this.

3 dried Chinese mushrooms

1.5 litres/2¼ pints chicken stock

125 g/4 oz cooked small prawns, peeled and cleaned

125 g/4 oz uncooked chicken, sliced into slivers

125 g/4 oz water chestnuts, sliced

125 g/4 oz bamboo shoots, sliced into matchsticks

60 g/2 oz fresh or frozen peas

2 tablespoons rice wine or dry sherry

½ teaspoon ground white pepper or to taste

2 teaspoons sesame oil or to taste

vegetable oil for deep-frying

1½–2 cups of rice crust (see method), broken into small pieces

Soak the dried mushrooms in warm water for 10 minutes. Drain, squeeze out the excess water, then remove and discard the stems. Slice the mushroom caps thinly.

Pour the chicken stock into a stock pot or large saucepan and bring to a boil on high heat.

Add the mushrooms, prawns, chicken, water chestnuts, bamboo shoots and peas. Cook for 2–3 minutes. Add the sherry, white pepper and sesame oil. Keep the soup warm while you prepare the rice.

Heat the oil in a wok, deep skillet or frying pan. The oil must be very hot, but not smoky. Carefully drop chunks of the rice crust into the hot oil and quickly deep-fry for about 1 minute or until golden. Using a slotted spoon, remove the rice pieces from the oil and place them on paper towels to drain off excess oil. Transfer soup to a warmed serving bowl. Add the rice to the hot soup while both are still hot. Serve immediately.

Rice Crust

If you have no rice crust, next time you cook rice, leave a thin layer of rice at the bottom of your cooking pot, sprinkle with 1 teaspoon oil or melted butter and leave the pot uncovered. Continue to cook the leftover rice on very low heat until it dries out and browns lightly. This can take up to an hour. Remember, the idea is to turn it crunchy and golden brown, not to char-burn it bitter, so keep a close eye on it! When ready, remove from the heat and allow it to cool. Peel it from the bottom of the cooking pot and store it in the freezer until needed.

Corn Soup

SERVES 4–6

Corn is a North American staple, so it would be almost unthinkable not to include at least one of the many corn soup recipes here. Ironically, the Native Americans who gave the world corn thought of the Chinese as another tribe, and so left them alone. I had a memorable corn soup in Chinatown in San Francisco many years ago, and I have loved the soup ever since.

375 g/12 oz boneless chicken breast, skinned and finely chopped

I egg white

I litre/2 pints chicken stock

450 g/I lb can creamed corn or sweetcorn kernels

2 tablespoons finely chopped lean ham (optional)

I egg, lightly beaten with a fork

2 tablespoons cornflour, blended with 2 tablespoons cold water

I teaspoon sesame oil or to taste

I spring onion complete with green top, very finely chopped

For the seasoning:

I teaspoon rice wine or dry sherry

2 teaspoons soy sauce

I teaspoon peeled and very finely chopped fresh root ginger

I teaspoon tapioca starch or potato flour

I teaspoon sesame oil

¹/₂ teaspoon ground white pepper

Mix the chicken, egg white and seasoning ingredients together in a large bowl. Cover and set aside to marinate for 15–20 minutes.

Boil the chicken stock in a large saucepan or cooking pot. Add the corn and immediately stir in the seasoned chicken. Keep stirring to prevent the chicken pieces from sticking together. Add the ham (if using) and continue cooking until the chicken turns white, about 1–2 minutes.

Lower the heat. Swirl in the beaten egg, add the blended cornflour and stir to thicken.

Drizzle a little sesame oil on top, sprinkle with the chopped spring onion and serve hot.

Beef and Asparagus in Black Bean Sauce

SERVES 3–4

The Chinese make a little go a long way, and it is always tastefully done. A piece of steak of the size served individually in New York or Texas could be turned by a Chinese cook into a sumptuous meal for four. The steak would be sliced into thin strips, seasoned and teamed with a finely chopped assortment of vegetables and sauces and, hey presto, a healthy meal fit for a banquet. This style of economical and healthy cooking has helped Chinese cooking gain popularity in North America.

500 g/1 lb lean beef steak (topside or rump)

500 g/1 lb asparagus

2 teaspoons vegetable oil

1 onion, peeled and very thinly sliced

180 ml/6 fl oz chicken stock

1 tablespoon cornflour, blended with 2 tablespoons cold water

For the marinade:

1 tablespoon soy sauce

1 teaspoon peeled and finely chopped fresh root ginger

2 tablespoons rice wine or dry sherry

1/2 teaspoon caster sugar

1 teaspoon cornflour

For the black bean sauce:

1 heaped tablespoon fermented black beans, well rinsed and drained

2–3 garlic cloves, peeled and finely chopped

1 tablespoon soy sauce

2 teaspoons rice wine or dry sherry

1/2 teaspoon caster sugar

1 teaspoon hot chilli oil (optional)

Trim off and discard any excess fat from the meat. Cut the meat across the grain into 3.5 cm/1 1/2 inch pieces and place in a large bowl. Combine all the ingredients for the marinade and stir into the beef. Cover and marinate for about 15 minutes.

Prepare the black bean sauce: mash the black beans and garlic to a pulp. Stir in the remaining ingredients and blend well.

Snap off the lower, tough portion of the asparagus and cut diagonally into thin pieces.

Heat 1 teaspoon of the oil in the wok and and gently swirl it around to coat the inside. Stir-fry the asparagus for about 1 minute, remove and set aside. Remove beef from the marinade. Reheat the wok with the remaining oil and once again gently swirl it around to coat the inside. Stir-fry the onion, then the beef for a few minutes, before adding the black bean sauce and beef marinade; cook for a further 3–4 minutes.

Add the asparagus to the wok and mix with the beef and vegetables. Add the stock and bring to the boil. Form a well in the centre, pour in the blended cornflour and quickly stir it in to mix. Lower the heat a little and continue cooking until the sauce thickens, about 2–3 minutes. Serve hot, with rice or noodles.

Steamed Chicken with Red Wolfberries

SERVES 4–6

According to Chinese medicine, wolfberries are good for cleansing the blood and for good vision. Shirley and I cooked this dish in Uncle Henry's house in San Francisco one afternoon while her family, daughter Kristina and mother Connie, prepared their own feast of potstickers (page 53). Shirley told me that she first steamed food this particular way by accident. She was teaching a Chinese cookery class when she realized she had forgotten to bring her steamer rack, so out of necessity she improvised by putting two chopsticks horizontally down into the wok of water as support for her bowl – she was then able to steam the contents of the bowl by resting it on the chopsticks. I liked her pragmatic approach.

2 whole chicken breasts or 2 drumsticks or legs

4 red Chinese dates

8 dried Chinese mushrooms

125 g/4 oz fresh root ginger

2 spring onions

2 Chinese sausages, cut into thin diagonal slices

4 fresh water chestnuts, cut into thin slices

60 g/2 oz dried red Chinese wolfberries, or fresh raspberries or blackberries

2 teaspoons sweet soy sauce

For the marinade:

2 tablespoons cornflour or tapioca powder, blended with 2 tablespoons water

2 tablespoons soy sauce

2 tablespoons oyster sauce

2 tablespoons rice wine or dry sherry

2 teaspoons sugar

¹/₂ teaspoon salt

Trim off the excess fat from the chicken. Using a cleaver, chop through the bones to cut the chicken into even, bite-size portions. Discard the skin if you wish. Put the chicken pieces in a large bowl, cover and set aside.

In another bowl, combine all ingredients for the marinade and stir to mix well. Pour over the chicken pieces. Stir to coat all the pieces of chicken in the marinade. Cover and marinate for 3–4 hours, the longer the better.

Soak the dates in hot water until soft. Remove and discard the pips, then cut the dates into small pieces. Soak the mushrooms in hot water for 10 minutes and watch them expand and come to life! Drain when fully expanded, squeeze out the excess water, then remove and discard the stems. Leave the mushroom caps whole.

Peel the ginger, then cut it into fine matchsticks or julienne. Chop the white bulbs of the spring onions very small with the side of a cleaver. Slice the stems and green tops of the onions diagonally into 2.5 cm/1 inch lengths.

Place 2 chopsticks or a steamer rack in a large wok. Fill with enough water to almost reach the chopsticks or rack. Arrange the pieces of chicken in a deep, heatproof ceramic or other dish, then scatter the other ingredients out attractively on top – first the dates, then the mushrooms, ginger, onions, sausages and water chestnuts. Finally, add the wolfberries and sprinkle with the soy sauce.

Bring the water in the wok to a boil and place the dish of chicken on the rack.

Cover and steam for about 40–50 minutes, or until the chicken meat is cooked and has turned white. Remove from the heat and serve hot, directly from the dish, with steamed or fried rice.

Fish Fillets in Wine Sauce

SERVES 3–4

1 kg/2 lb any firm white fish fillets (eg halibut or sole), cut into 5 x 2.5 cm/2 x 1 inch pieces

vegetable oil for deep-frying

2 egg whites, lightly beaten with a fork

3 tablespoons cornflour

3 tablespoons vegetable oil

2 teaspoons caster sugar

125 ml/4 fl oz dry white wine

60 ml/2 fl oz rice wine

1 teaspoon salt

2 tablespoons cornflour, blended with 180 ml/6 fl oz cold fish stock

---

The Meaning of Fish
A whole fish represents togetherness and abundance.

Clean and rinse the pieces of fish in cold water. Pat them dry with paper towels.

In a small heavy-based and deep skillet or frying pan, heat up the oil for deep-frying on medium heat.

When the oil is hot, dip each piece of fish in the beaten egg whites, then dredge it through the cornflour to thoroughly coat it. Deep-fry each piece quickly to crisp the outside, about 1 minute each. Remove from the oil and drain off the excess oil on paper towels. Continue until all the fish is fried. Set aside.

Heat the 3 tablespoons oil in a wok on medium heat and gently swirl it around to coat the inside. Add the sugar, wines and salt, stirring all the time, then add the blended cornflour and stir until the sauce thickens. Carefully arrange the fish pieces in the sauce in the wok and turn them over a few times to coat them with the sauce. Serve hot, with rice or noodles tossed through with colourful Chinese vegetables.

Ma Po Tofu

SERVES 4–6

My Chinese American friend, Shirley Fong Torres, gave me this recipe. She says *ma po* means "pock-marked" or "old woman's tofu", apparently based on the old Chinese woman who created it for her husband. Their house was situated between the butcher and the tofu shop, so she made him lamb and tofu dishes. Tofu, or bean curd, is bland. It needs to be put with other foods so it will absorb their flavours into its rich fabric to give a meal texture and substance.

1 tablespoon vegetable oil

250 g/8 oz lean minced pork

1 teaspoon peeled and grated fresh root ginger

4 garlic cloves, peeled and finely chopped

3–4 whole ripe chillies, de-seeded and finely chopped

2 tablespoons soy sauce

2 tablespoons brown bean sauce

250 ml/8 fl oz chicken stock

3 teaspoons cornflour, blended with 1 tablespoon cold water

2 teaspoons sesame oil

400 g/14 oz tofu, fresh or fried, cut into bite-size pieces

1/2 teaspoon hot chilli oil

3 tablespoons finely chopped spring onions

Heat 2 teaspoons of the vegetable oil in a wok and gently swirl it around to coat the inside. Stir-fry the pork over high heat, making sure to break it up, until it browns. Remove with a slotted spoon and drain on paper towels.

Put the rest of the vegetable oil in the wok and reheat it until the wok gets smoky. Add the ginger, garlic and chillies. Cook for 30 seconds, then add the soy sauce, brown bean sauce and pork. Stir-fry for about 30 seconds, add the chicken stock and bring to a boil, then stir in the blended cornflour. Lower the heat a little. Add the sesame oil and tofu and gently stir them into mix. Cook on medium to low heat for about 5–10 minutes. Finally, add the hot chilli oil and a dash more sesame oil to taste. Top with the spring onions and serve hot, with rice.

Tofu

In the health-conscious Californian culture, tofu is gaining momentum. A good source of concentrated protein, with a solid texture, it makes an economical and healthy substitute for meat. It is sold in slabs of compacted solids, a product of soy milk curds. Although production machines are modern, the process of manufacture is traditional. Tofu has no chemicals, preservatives or cholesterol, and it is low in calories and high in protein. It comes in many versatile textures: soft for soups, medium for stir-frying and soups, and firm for stuffing and stir-frying.

Pork Spareribs with Black Bean Sauce

SERVES 4–6 AS A SIDE DISH

Among the myriad of different delicious Chinese dishes on offer in the United States, there are a few creations sold more for their commercial viability than their authenticity. Dishes like chop suey, chow mein, sweet and sour pork and spareribs. The size of the ribs on offer in most takeaway shops alone depicts a culture other than that of the Chinese, whose pork spareribs are cut much smaller by comparison.

750 g /1 ¹/₂ lb Chinese-style pork spareribs, cut into 2.5 cm/ 1 inch pieces

1 tablespoon vegetable oil

1 onion, peeled and diced into 2.5 cm/1 inch pieces

250 ml/8 fl oz chicken or vegetable stock

1 tablespoon cornflour, blended with 1 tablespoon cold water

¹/₂ red and ¹/₂ green pepper (capsicums), diced into squares

soy sauce (optional)

For the black bean sauce:

2 tablespoons fermented black beans, well rinsed and drained

2 garlic cloves, peeled and finely chopped

1 teaspoon peeled and finely chopped fresh root ginger

1 tablespoon soy sauce

1 teaspoon rice wine or dry sherry

¹/₂ teaspoon caster sugar

Half fill a large cooking pot with water. Bring the water to a boil, add the spareribs and boil on high heat for about 4–5 minutes to get rid of excess fat. Remove from the heat, drain away the water and rinse the pork in cold water. Set the ribs aside.

Make the black bean sauce: combine the black beans and garlic together and mash into a smoothish pulp. Add the ginger, soy sauce, wine or sherry and the sugar.

Heat the oil in a wok and gently swirl it around to coat the inside. Stir-fry the onion and spareribs over high heat for 2–3 minutes. Add the black bean sauce and stir until the ribs are coated with it.
Add the stock and cook over high heat for 1 minute, then lower the heat and simmer for 20 minutes or until the meat is tender. Stir in the blended cornflour and the peppers and cook for a further 3 minutes or until the peppers are tender and the sauce has thickened. Taste and add some more soy sauce if you wish. Serve hot, as a side dish.

Kung Pao Prawns

SERVES 3–4

This is one of my favourite Chinese meals, served with steaming hot jasmine rice. The bonus is that it cooks really quickly and is easy to prepare.

500 g/1 lb fresh peeled raw prawns

1 egg white

2 teaspoons soy sauce

1 teaspoon rice wine or dry sherry

½ teaspoon white pepper

2 tablespoons vegetable oil

4–5 dried red chillies

1 onion, peeled and thinly sliced

1 green pepper (capsicum), de-seeded and diced into bite-size pieces

60 g/2 oz bamboo shoots, sliced into matchsticks

2 spring onions with green tops, cut into 2.5 cm/1 inch pieces

125 g/4 oz roasted unsalted peanuts

1 tablespoon cornflour, blended with 2 tablespoons cold water

½ teaspoon sesame oil

For the seasoning sauce:

2 garlic cloves, peeled and finely chopped

2 tablespoons soy sauce

1 teaspoon oyster sauce

1 teaspoon rice wine or dry sherry

125 ml/4 fl oz chicken or vegetable stock

De-vein the prawns: cut down the line of the spine with a sharp knife just deep enough to expose the vein without cutting right through the prawn. Remove and discard this vein, then wash the prawns and pat them dry.

Put the prawns in a bowl, add the egg white, soy sauce, wine or sherry and the white pepper and toss through.

Mix together all the ingredients for the seasoning sauce and set aside.

Heat the oil in a wok and gently swirl it around to coat the inside. When the wok is very hot, stir-fry the chillies until they are dark, remove and set aside. Quickly stir-fry together the prawns, onion, pepper, bamboo shoots and spring onions for about 1 minute or until the prawns change colour and the onions turn translucent.

Add the seasoning sauce and stir-fry for another 30 seconds before you add the peanuts. Stir well, and finally add the blended cornflour. Cook until the sauce thickens. Sprinkle on the sesame oil, then stir well to mix and heat through. Serve hot, with steaming hot jasmine or other aromatic rice.

Stir-Fried Chinese Green Vegetables

SERVES 3–4

Chinese cooks use lots of vegetables, so despite the historical traumas and nightmares of the early Chinese settlers, the Californian climate must have given them some small comfort – a good environment for growing fresh produce all year round. Bok choy is a cross between celery and cabbage: its short and broad white stems resemble celery, while the solid broad green leaves resemble cabbage. The combination lends itself readily to many recipes. This one is Cantonese.

750 g/1 ½ lb bok choy

4 dried Chinese mushrooms

2 tablespoons vegetable oil

2 garlic cloves, peeled and very finely chopped

1 teaspoon peeled and very finely chopped fresh root ginger

1 medium onion, peeled and thinly sliced

1 teaspoon soy sauce

125 ml/4 fl oz chicken or vegetable stock

1 teaspoon cornflour, blended with 3 teaspoons cold water

½ teaspoon salt

Clean the bok choy and rinse it to get rid of all grit and dirt. Drain and cut into bite-size pieces.

Soak the mushrooms in hot water for 10 minutes. Drain, squeeze out the excess water, then remove and discard the stems. Cut each mushroom cap into three.

Heat the oil in a wok and gently swirl it around to coat the inside. Add the garlic, ginger and onion and stir-fry until the onion is translucent and the garlic and ginger are aromatic and fragrant. Add the mushrooms and stir-fry for a further 2 minutes.

Add the bok choy and toss on high heat to mix everything through. Finally, add the soy sauce and the stock, continuing to cook on high heat for 1 minute. Stir in the blended cornflour, sprinkle with the salt and add more soy sauce if you like strong flavours. Serve hot, with fish, shellfish, meat, chicken, rice or noodles. Or serve by itself.

Immortal Mushrooms

Dried black Chinese mushrooms are preferred by Chinese chefs to fresh ones. Medicinal texts refer to them as "plants of immortality". The Japanese call them shiitake.

Stir-Fried Bean Sprouts

SERVES 2–3

Bean sprouts, the crunchy off-white shoots of mung beans, are easy to grow, healthy, tasty and bulk up any dish. When unexpected guests drop in, reach for the bean sprouts and noodles; when you feel like a light meal, reach for the bean sprouts and noodles; if you are too busy with no time for elaborate meals, reach for the bean sprouts . . . you can see why this has caught on so well in California, the land of diets. It is a good recipe to have in your back pocket.

2 teaspoons vegetable oil

2 eggs, lightly beaten with a fork

2 garlic cloves, peeled and finely chopped

250 g/8 oz cooked Chinese-style roast pork, finely chopped (optional)

2 spring onions, cut into 2.5 cm/1 inch lengths

250 g/8 oz Chinese yellow chives, cut into 2.5 cm/1 inch lengths

500 g/1 lb fresh bean sprouts

90 ml/3 fl oz vegetable or chicken stock

1 tablespoon soy sauce

1/4 teaspoon ground white pepper

1/2 teaspoon sesame oil

Heat 1 teaspoon of the oil in a wok and gently swirl it around to coat the inside. When smoky, stir-fry the eggs on high heat into an omelette. Remove the omelette, cut it into strips and set it aside. Reheat the wok with the remaining oil. Add the garlic, roast pork (if using), spring onions and Chinese chives. Stir-fry for 30 seconds before you add the bean sprouts. Stir for 1 minute, then add the stock and soy sauce. Keep stirring until the bean sprouts reduce in volume.

Return the egg to the wok and mix well. Finally, sprinkle white pepper and sesame oil over the vegetables and egg and toss through. Serve hot, tossed through steamed noodles as a light meal, or by itself as a meal in its own right.

Vegetarian Potstickers

KUO TIEHS

MAKES ABOUT 20

When I first heard the word potstickers applied to the tiny Chinese dough parcels often filled with anything from seafood to pork to vegetables, I thought it sounded distinctly American. Well, I was wrong. The northern Chinese version of these food parcels are called *kuo tiehs*, which means "stuck to the pot". Different parts of China have different names for potstickers, but the commonest name outside China is wuntun, which means "swallowing a cloud". To see them steamed and floating in clear soups, I guess they must resemble clouds.

4 dried Chinese mushrooms

500 g/1 lb potsticker wrappers (available at most Asian stores)

about 4 teaspoons vegetable oil

500 ml/16 fl oz vegetable stock

For the filling:

250 g /8 oz spinach leaves

125 g/4 oz Chinese cabbage, shredded

125 g/4 oz bamboo shoots or water chestnuts

125 g/4 oz pressed bean curd

30 g/1 oz cloud ear fungus

1 teaspoon finely chopped spring onion

1 teaspoon peeled and finely chopped fresh root ginger

2 garlic cloves, peeled and chopped 2 teaspoons soy sauce

1 teaspoon rice wine or dry sherry 1 teaspoon cornflour

1/2 teaspoon sesame oil

a pinch of ground white pepper

Soak the mushrooms in hot water for 10 minutes. Drain, squeeze out the excess water, then remove and discard the stems. Cut each mushroom cap into three.

For the filling, all the vegetables need to be very finely chopped. This is time-comsuming by hand, so I suggest processing them in a food processor, taking care not to blend too smoothly so they still retain some texture. Put the chopped vegetables in a bowl, stir in the remaining filling ingredients, cover and refrigerate until needed.

Assemble the potstickers: place a spoonful of filling in the centre of each wrapper. Moisten around the filling, then draw the wrapper together over the filling and press together to seal the filling inside and form a little parcel. Repeat until all the wrappers are used and the filling is finished. Set each potsticker upright on a plate to give it a base.

Heat up a non-stick skillet or frying pan and add 3 teaspoons oil. Arrange the potstickers close together in the skillet and fry the bottoms until they brown. Pour enough stock into the skillet to cover the lower halves of the potstickers, then cover the pan and cook on medium heat for about 7–8 minutes or until the liquid evaporates.

Slowly ease the potstickers out of the pan, adding a little oil to help if necessary. Arrange the cooked potsickers on a serving dish and garnish as you wish. Serve with an assortment of sauces like rice vinegar, soy sauce, hot chilli oil, tomato sauce, savoury black bean oil, etc.

Fresh Spinach with Fermented Bean Curd

SERVES 2–3

Fermented bean curd is readily available at Chinese and other Asian stores. It is soaked in water, wine and spices, etc, and has a strong flavour. It is an acquired taste, so use it judiciously.

1 tablespoon vegetable oil

6 garlic cloves, peeled and finely chopped

2 teaspoons fermented bean curd, or more according to taste

500 g/1 lb fresh spinach, cut into 5 cm/2 inch lengths

60 ml/2 fl oz chicken stock

2 teaspoons soy sauce

¹⁄₂ teaspoon sesame oil

Heat the oil in a wok and gently swirl it around to coat the inside. Add the garlic and stir-fry until it turns golden. Add the fermented bean curd and stir-fry for a few seconds, then add the spinach and stock. Continue to stir-fry on high heat for another 30 seconds until the spinach reduces in volume and goes bright green. Add the soy sauce and sesame oil and toss through. Serve hot, with other dishes.

Almond Tea

SERVES 4–6

This is a beverage and not, strictly speaking, a tea as we know it. It is a refreshing drink nonetheless.

125 g/4 oz sugar

1 litre/2 pints water

125 g/4 oz finely ground almonds

125 g/4 oz finely ground rice

In a heavy, preferably non-stick saucepan, dissolve the sugar in the water as you bring it to the boil. Throw in the rice and almonds. Remove from the heat and allow to infuse until the liquid is cold. Strain the liquid through cheesecloth. Adjust the sweetness if necessary. Chill before serving, by itself or with ice-cream.

Almond Jelly

Make the Almond Tea as opposite. To 1 cup of the Tea, stir in 45 g/1 ½ oz powdered gelatine and allow it to soften for 5 minutes.

In a small saucepan, heat a further 1 cup of the Tea and dissolve the softened gelatine in it over a low heat. Add this to the rest of the cooled Tea. Pour into a shallow dish and leave to set.

Cut the jelly into triangles and serve by itself or with ice-cream.

Fried Fruits

SERVES 3–4

2 large apples
juice of 1 lemon
oil for deep-frying
2 tablespoons caster sugar
2 teaspoons ground cinnamon
thick cream, to serve

For the batter:
250 g/8 oz cornflour
250 g/8 oz plain flour
1 egg
1 teaspoon baking powder

First make the batter: combine all the ingredients in a mixing bowl and blend either by hand or in a blender, with enough cold water to make a thin batter. Place in the refrigerator for 20–30 minutes before use.

When ready, peel the apples, then cut them horizontally into 5 mm/¼ inch thick rounds. It is easier to core them once sliced into rounds like this. Core them, then dip each slice in the lemon juice to preserve its colour.

Heat up the oil in heavy-based, preferably non-stick, skillet or frying pan. When the oil is hot, dip a few apple slices in the batter to coat them all over. Gently lower them into the hot oil and deep-fry both sides until golden, about 30-40 seconds each side. Remove from the oil and drain on paper towels. Keep in a preheated warm oven until all the fruit slices have been fried. Mix the sugar and cinnamon and sprinkle over the fried apple slices. Serve hot, topped with cream.

German American Tastes

Bratwurst sausage earrings in New Ulm

Sit down in any diner in America and the chances are that you will be eating German food. Every American has eaten or heard of frankfurters (hot dogs), hamburgers, sauerkraut, torte, lager, strudel, cookies, pretzels and doughnuts. America's taste for sweet pastries, cakes and puddings comes from the kitchens of Germany and Holland – although many German Americans today will say that they find modern American food too sweet for them. The American love for sweet-sour dishes, meat served with fruit such as applesauce, noodles, dumplings, pickles, schnitzel, potato salads and cheesecakes, are all testimony to the enduring traditions of the German-speaking people, who have journeyed from all parts of Middle Europe to find a new life in America. A journey that started as long ago as 1682, when William Penn established a colony in what is now Pennsylvania as a refuge for "the persecuted and oppressed people of Europe". Settlers in this com-

munity are usually referred to as Pennsylvania Dutch, which has led to confusion with immigrants from Holland. It is believed that the name came from the German word *Deutsch*, meaning German.

Poverty among the rural communities was another powerful force that sent thousands on the long and dangerous journey to the New World in search of land they could farm and call their own. There were also German mercenaries hired by the King of England, political exiles, intellectuals and artists. By the start of the American Revolution, a quarter of a million Germans were already settled in America. They had come from as far afield as Baden, Franconia, the Palatine, Alsace and German-speaking Bohemia and Switzerland. They spread across the new continent and created their own German communities in Pennsylvania and New York in the northeast, the Carolinas and Virginia in the south, California and Texas in the southwest, and in the great farming heartland states of America, such as Iowa, Wisconsin and Minnesota.

The last major group of German immigrants to the United States came following the First and Second World Wars. They were German-speaking displaced peoples from Pomerania, Silesia, Prussia, Poland, Hungary, Slovakia, Yugoslavia, Sudetenland, Romania and Russia. Their background, culture, music and food are, of course, very varied, but they all preserved their language, customs and traditions, adopting some elements of the American region in which they settled and, in turn, influencing it. They developed thriving cultural institutions – academic, literary, religious, artistic and culinary.

My own travels took me to find German cooking in Minnesota in the Midwest. I visited families preparing for their summer Heritagefest in the state's most German city, New Ulm. It is alleged to be the least diverse town in the whole United States, since most of its 14,000 residents are of German descent – either from the German province of Württemberg, whose principal city is Ulm, or from the German-speaking borderlands of Bohemia – what is now the Czech Republic.

True to form, New Ulm proudly boasts its own brewery producing different varieties of beer using traditional German recipes handed down through generations, and its own home-made sausage shop producing bratwurst, bologna, cervelat, kielbasa, wiener, knackwurst and bockwurst, to name just a few.

The Minnesota-born writer, Sinclair Lewis, described the landscape in which he grew up as, "a glorious country, a land to be big in", and I came across a popular Pennsylvania Dutch saying which amused me: "Better a burst stomach than wasted food".

These are two popular quotations I can really understand, although I think Rudyard Kipling was pushing his luck when he described German American farmers and their "fat farms, fat cattle and fat women". If many German Americans are, like me, a little on the large side, it could be because their diet was originally designed to help them survive hard work, poverty and cold.

When the mainly rural German settlers arrived in Minnesota, they saw a landscape that was both big and familiar. Forests, lakes and huge flat prairies of rich black earth reminded them of their homeland, where they had been denied land which was normally owned by the nobility. Life in America for those early settlers was very tough. The winters were as hard and long as those in their homeland, but at least the knowledge they brought with them about ways to preserve the meat, fruit and vegetables by salting, drying, curing, smoking and preserving in vinegar was invaluable. Every last bit of the pig was turned into ham and sausages, cabbage was made into sauerkraut, apples were dried, and fish steeped in brine. Hospitality grew out of hardship and companionship and support are still a big feature of life in Minnesota. Neighbours will always call round in time of need with a "hotdish", a hearty dish of whatever is to hand pulled together with cans of soup. If the forecast says heavy snow, everyone gets together in one house with plenty of good home cooking and beer to "have a good time until the thaw".

Many German American recipes go back deep into the past. Many others developeed from old-world dishes that have travelled in new directions – when early settlers discovered the new foods they could freely hunt and cultivate, they began to experiment with new ingredients. Despite the historic hardships, the German American communities remain tightly knit. They have a strong reliance on their land, each other and their traditional foods and festivals. These serve to give them an extra affinity with the life that they left behind.

Getting to grips with 2000lbs of potatoes for German Potato Salad at the Heritage fest in New Ulm, Minnesota

Cold Fruit Soup

SERVES 4–6

500 g/1 lb apples, cherries or other fruit of your choice, peeled, cored or de-seeded as appropriate and chopped into pieces

2 litres/4 pints water

1 tablespoon cornflour

125 ml/4 fl oz apple juice, cherry juice or water

2 tablespoons sugar

2 tablespoons fresh lemon juice

125 ml/4 fl oz white wine

Set a small portion of fruit aside in the refrigerator for garnish. Cook the rest of the fruit in the water for about 15–20 minutes (depending on the fruit) until soft. Remove from the heat and allow to cool a little, then pureé in a blender or push through a sieve, reserving the juice.

Blend the cornflour with the fruit juice or water. Put the fruit purée in a saucepan and bring to a boil. Stir in the blended cornflour and mix until smooth and blended into the hot soup. Stir in the sugar, lemon juice and wine. Turn off the heat and allow the soup to cool. Refrigerate until chilled. Serve cold, garnished with the reserved fruit.

Pea Soup

SERVES 4–6

500 g/1 lb split green or yellow peas

1 big ham bone with lots of meat on it

1 large onion, peeled and finely chopped

1 medium leek, thinly sliced 3 large carrots, diced

2 celery sticks complete with leaves, finely chopped

1 teaspoon fresh, chopped marjoram or sage

1/2 teaspoon ground allspice

2 bay leaves

salt and pepper to taste

1.5 litres/3 pints water

3 tablespoons cornflour, blended with 90 ml/3 fl oz water

2–3 tablespoons chopped fresh parsley, to garnish

Wash the peas, then soak in lots of tap water overnight to soften them. The soaking water should be at least 5 cm/2 inches above the level of the peas.

The next day, drain the peas and rinse under the cold tap. Pour the peas into a big soup pot and add the ham bone, onion, leek, carrots, celery, marjoram or sage, allspice, bay leaves and salt and pepper to taste. Pour in the 1.5 litres/3 pints water and bring to a boil. Reduce the heat to medium, cover and cook for 2 hours, adding more water if necessary. Turn off the heat and allow the soup to cool a little.

Remove the bay leaves and ham bone from the soup. Cut off all the meat from the bone and chop it into small pieces; set aside. Discard the bone and the bay leaves. Purée the soup in a blender until smooth, then return it to the soup pot. Stir the blended cornflour to ensure it is smooth, then pour it into the soup and heat, stirring, until the soup thickens. Add the pieces of chopped ham, and taste and adjust seasoning. Serve hot, garnished with chopped fresh parsley.

Hoppel Poppel

SERVES 6–8

Farm work is heavy and demanding, and one needs a lot of stamina and something substantial in the stomach before tackling the tasks. This tasty German American breakfast is designed for just such a purpose.

125 ml/4 fl oz corn or other vegetable oil

8 small potatoes, partly cooked and cut into thick slices

6 tablespoons butter

1 large onion, peeled and finely chopped

250 g/8 oz green pepper (capsicum), de-seeded and diced

180 g/6 oz mushrooms, thickly sliced

250 g/8 oz all-beef salami, preferably German, sliced

10 eggs, well beaten

2 tablespoons milk

2 tablespoons chopped fresh parsley

250 g/8 oz Cheddar cheese, grated

salt and pepper to taste

Heat the oil in a skillet or frying pan and fry the potato slices until they turn brown. Add half the butter, the onion and green pepper and fry for about 2 minutes on medium heat. Add the mushrooms and salami and continue cooking and stirring until the vegetables become limp, the salami crusty and the potatoes crisp.

Melt the rest of the butter and combine it with the eggs, milk and parsley, whisk quickly and pour over the potatoes. Continue cooking and, as the eggs start to set, sprinkle the top with the cheese. Cover and cook, without stirring, for 5–6 minutes or until the eggs are well set but still soft. Be careful not to overcook and dry out the eggs. Serve immediately, with muffins, bagels or buttered toast and a hot drink.

Pork Ribs and Sauerkraut

SERVES 4–6

750 g/1 1/2 lb sauerkraut

2 cooking apples, cored and sliced

2 tablespoons sugar

1 teaspoon caraway seeds

2 kg/4 lb spareribs, separated into individual pieces

salt and pepper to season

Pre-heat the oven to 150°C/300°F/Gas Mark 2.

Rinse the sauerkraut quickly in cold water. Drain.

Mix together the sauerkraut, apples, sugar and caraway seeds in a large cooking pot. Season the ribs generously with salt and pepper. Arrange the ribs neatly on top of the sauerkraut mix. Bake in the oven for 4-5 hours or until cooked through. Serve hot.

Bratwurst in Ale

SERVES 4–6

Germany has the largest variety of sausages and bratwurst is one of its many big ones. The best-looking bratwurst I ever saw were in New Ulm, Minnesota, in the sausage shop owned by Lenny Donahue, who specialises in German meats. So good were these sausages, I was determined to fashion ear-rings out of them so I can carry my own regular supplies!

I litre/2 pints water

750 g/1 ¹/₂ lb bratwurst

90 g/3 oz butter

2 bay leaves

500 ml/16 fl oz light ale

I large onion, peeled and finely chopped

30 g/1 oz plain flour

salt and pepper to taste

2 teaspoons caster sugar (optional)

chopped fresh parsley, to garnish

In a large saucepan, bring the water to a boil. Prick the sausage all over and carefully lower it into the boiling water. Boil on medium heat for about 5–7 minutes. Drain off the water and discard.

Add half the butter to the sausage, increase the heat and brown the outside very quickly all over. Lower the heat to medium and add the bay leaves and half the ale. Cover and simmer until the ale has reduced to half its volume.

Meanwhile, in a skillet or frying pan, make a light brown roux: melt the remaining butter, fry the chopped onion until golden, then stir in the flour and continue stirring and cooking until the mixture turns light brown. Quickly blend in the remaining ale, stirring all the time to form a light and creamy smooth sauce. Season with salt and pepper and add to the sausage mixture. Taste and add the sugar (if using). Stir well to mix and make sure the sausage is well coated with the sauce. Simmer on low heat until the sausage is cooked and the sauce thickens. Garnish with chopped parsley and serve hot, with sautéed or boiled cabbage and potatoes of your choice.

Sauerbraten

SERVES 6–8

Sauerbraten is a German-style substantial beef pot roast. It is a dish you look forward to, not a dish you prepare and eat on the same day. Everybody's grandmother has got an old recipe for sauerbraten, it's been loved that long. The meat has to marinate for at least 3–5 days, even before the cooking starts, so it is definitely one of those dishes that tastes better with age.

For the marinade:

375 ml/12 fl oz red wine

375 ml/12 fl oz water

4 garlic cloves, peeled and left whole

1 medium onion, finely chopped

2 bay leaves

1 teaspoon peppercorns

60 g/2 oz sugar

For the roast:

1.5 kg/3 lb rump or shoulder of beef

1 carrot, cut into chunks

1 celery stick, thickly sliced

1 medium onion, peeled and spiked with 3 peeled garlic cloves

For the gravy:

1 teaspoon bouillon granules or 1 stock cube

125 ml/4 fl oz red wine

1 teaspoon ground ginger

1 teaspoon salt

3 tablespoons cornflour

125 ml/4 fl oz sour cream

Heat all the ingredients for the marinade together in a large stock pot. Do not boil or the alcohol will evaporate. Stir until the sugar dissolves. Put the meat to be roasted in a large container and add enough marinade for the meat to be immersed halfway. Save the remaining marinade for later. Cover the meat, allow to cool and refrigerate for 4 days. Turn the meat twice a day, to ensure the marinade reaches all parts.

On the fifth day, lift the roast from the marinade and place it in a large heavy-based casserole dish or similar cooking pot. Pour the marinade from the meat and the reserved marinade over the top of the roast.

Add the carrot, celery and garlic-spiked onion. Bring to a boil, turn the heat down to low and cook for 4–6 hours or until the meat is very tender. Alternatively, the covered pot can be placed in a low oven for 4–6 hours.

Make the gravy: carefully lift the roast out of the cooking pot and set aside. Skim off any fat from the sauce and discard. Pour 500 ml/16 fl oz of the sauce into a smaller saucepan. Add the bouillon granules, wine, ginger and salt and bring to a boil. Blend the cornflour with 60 ml/2 fl oz water and slowly blend it into the sauce, stirring slowly. Continue to boil for 1–2 minutes, then lower the heat.

Slice the roast and arrange on a platter with the vegetables all around. Pour half the hot gravy carefully over the whole lot. Mix the other half of the gravy with the sour cream and serve separately, accompanied by potatoes, noodles or dumplings.

Swabian Noodles

SERVES 4–6

These really tiny, home-made spaghetti are called *Spätzle* in German, which means "little sparrows". They are very popular served by themselves with cheese or as accompaniments to savoury dishes, but they can also be teamed with egg custard, sugar, etc and turned into quick desserts as well. On occasion, they are served as a replacement for dumplings in soups, or are fried and used as an attractive garnish. I must confess, the little sparrows are not as easy to make as it first seems!

500 g/1 lb plain flour
1 teaspoon baking powder
1 ½ teaspoons salt
4 eggs, well beaten
2 litres/4 pints water

Mix the flour, baking powder, ½ teaspoon salt and all the eggs together, then add a little of the water at a time until a soft malleable dough is formed.

Bring the remaining water and salt to a boil in a large saucepan. The traditional way of making spätzle is to push the dough through a colander with a wooden spoon. It is helpful if your colander, sieve or ricer is chilled before pressing the dough through because this keeps the dough cool and helps the noodles form firmly and quickly. It is not always easy to achieve, so chill your tools beforehand.

Put small portions of the dough in the chilled colander, sieve or ricer and, using a cold wooden spoon, firmly push the dough through the holes to (hopefully) extrude short strings of noodle into the salted boiling water. Boil the spätzle for just 3 minutes until they rise to the top of the water, then scoop them out with a slotted spoon into a dish and mix them with a teaspoonful of butter to stop them from sticking together. Keep the spätzle warm until all the dough is cooked in the same way. Serve hot.

Variations
There are two other ways you might prefer to cook your noodles.
1. Roll the dough out on a floured board into long, very thin sausages, cut into 2.5–5 cm/1–2 inch lengths and cook in the boiling water. They can be served like this, or you can fry them after boiling in melted butter until golden all over.
2. Cut off pieces of dough (matchstick-style or size according to preference) and drop them straight into the boiling water. Cook as above.

German Potato Salad

WÜRTTEMBERGER KARTOFFELSALAT

SERVES 4–6

In Germany, potatoes are an important side dish along with cabbage, in fact there are almost as many variations on preparing potatoes as there are German dialects. This potato salad recipe is one of Myrtle Brands', the type that's regular fare in most New Ulm homes. It's unlike the potato salad most people are used to, because it is sweet and warm.

1 tablespoon butter

1 tablespoon vegetable oil

250 g/8 oz bacon, cut into bite-sized pieces

3 medium onions, peeled and finely chopped

185 ml/6 fl oz water

60 g/2 oz sugar

60 ml/2 fl oz vinegar

2 tablespoons bacon grease or fat

1 tablespoon cornflour

salt and pepper to taste

1 kg/2 lb potatoes, freshly boiled and hot, thinly sliced or cubed

Heat the butter and oil in a heavy-based skillet or frying pan, add the bacon pieces and fry on low heat until cooked but not browned. Using a slotted spoon, remove the cooked bacon pieces and set aside.

Fry the onions in the same oil until transparent.

Drain off the oil into a saucepan, add 125 ml/4 fl oz of the water, the sugar and vinegar and bring to a boil.

Blend the cornflour and 1 teaspoon salt with the remaining water, then add it to the boiling liquid. Continue to boil until the mixture thickens. Stir in the onions, fried bacon and hot potatoes, and season to taste. Serve warm.

Sauerkraut Hot Dish

SERVES 4

"Hot Dish" is basically a casserole with noodles and canned soup as its base, with additions of frozen vegetables and some sort of meat (either minced steak or chicken) and sometimes a cheese topping. It is a real quickie standby for impromptu guests. Marlene Domeier, a local radio announcer, gave me this recipe.

3 tablespoons vegetable oil

500 g/1 lb minced hamburger steak

1 onion, peeled and very finely chopped

salt and pepper to taste

375 g/12 oz Swabian noodles (see p.62)

1 medium can cream of chicken soup

½ can water

Pre-heat the oven to 180°C/350°F/Gas 4.

Heat the oil in a heavy-based skillet or frying pan and brown the mince and onion, about 7-10 minutes. Season to taste with salt and pepper. Arrange at the bottom of a casserole, spread the noodles over the top, then the sauerkraut followed by the chicken soup and water. Bake in the oven for 1 hour. Serve hot.

Bread and Potato Dumplings

MAKES ABOUT 9

Meals are very generous all over the United States of America, but that notwithstanding, I still find meals in Minnesota even more generous again. This dumpling recipe was given to me by Dodie Wendinger. A great cook, she comes from an old German immigrant family and lives in St George with her extended family. The dumplings are quick and easy, and add texture to any soup or stew – simply drop them in for the last 20 minutes of the cooking time.

I medium loaf of white bread, crusts cut off and cubed

¹/₂ medium-size loaf of light rye bread, crusts cut off and cubed

5 potatoes, peeled and grated raw, including the juice

I teaspoon salt

about 125 ml/4 fl oz milk

water for boiling the dumplings

Mix all the first 4 ingredients together to make a firm dough. If necessary, add small amounts of milk to help hasten the process.

Bring lots of water to a boil in a casserole dish or large saucepan. Make 9 dumplings out of the dough and carefully drop them into the boiling water. Cook for 15 minutes or until cooked and risen to the top of the boiling water. Remove with a slotted spoon and serve with sauerkraut, or as you choose.

Variations

You may prefer to omit the bread and make just potato dumplings. In which case, finely grate 12 potatoes instead of 5, and add 250 g/8 oz plain flour, 2 teaspoons baking powder and 1 tablespoon salt. Form the dough into balls and cook as above. Another alternative is to make an all-potato dough, then roll and cut it into "Swabian potato finger dumplings". These are boiled first, then fried until lightly brown all over.

Opposite: Bratwurst in Ale (p.60) with Red Cabbage (p.66).
Following pages: Ma Po Tofu (p.48); Steamed Chicken with Red Wolfberries (p.46).

Potato Bread

KARTOFFELBROT

MAKES TWO MEDIUM LOAVES

Bread-making is not as popular as it once was, but those who bake generally make rye bread, pumpernickel bread and French loaves. This potato bread has obviously been around the USA. It is a slightly heavier bread and became one of my favourites when I visited Minnesota. It comes from an old Pennsylvania Dutch recipe.

2 teaspoons salt
625 ml/21 fl oz cold water
1 large potato, peeled and diced
1 tablespoon dried yeast
125 ml/4 fl oz warm water
30 g/1 oz butter or margarine
2 tablespoons sugar
1.5 kg/3 lb bread flour

Mix half the salt with the water and boil the diced potatoes until tender. Remove from the heat and mash the potatoes in their liquid. Cover and leave to stand for 10 minutes. Dissolve the yeast in the warm water and let stand for 10 minutes.

Add the butter or margarine, the sugar and remaining salt to the mashed potato. Blend together thoroughly. Slowly fold in half the flour a little at a time, then the yeast. Add the remaining flour and mix to a dough.

Flour a board, put the dough on the board and knead for about 10–15 minutes until elastic and smooth.

Lightly grease the top of the dough and place it in a lightly greased large container. Cover and leave to rise, about 45 minutes to 1 hour. Pre-heat the oven to 190°C/375°F/Gas 5.

Punch down the dough, divide into two halves and shape them to roughly the dimensions of your loaf tins. Place each piece in a 2 lb loaf tin. Shape to fit the tin, cover again and allow to stand for a further 30 minutes until proved and doubled in size. Bake in the oven for about 40 minutes.

Opposite: Apple Strudel (p.67).

Red Cabbage

ROTKRAUT

SERVES 6–8

Kraut, or cabbage, was first known in Europe over 4000 years ago for its apparent medicinal value. With progressive cultivation over the years, many different varieties have emerged, including the red cabbage. Cabbage has become so synonymous with German cooking that it simply had to emigrate to the Minnesota River Valley with the 18,000 Germans who arrived there in the 1850s.

1 large head of red cabbage

2 tablespoons bacon dripping or vegetable oil, according to personal taste

1 medium onion, peeled and finely chopped

2 small cooking apples, cored, peeled and thickly sliced

60 g/2 oz brown sugar

1 teaspoon salt

60 ml/2 fl oz red wine

5 tablespoons wine vinegar

1 tablespoon redcurrant jelly

Remove the outside leaves of the cabbage and discard. Wash the remaining cabbage and coarsely shred it. Melt the dripping or oil in a large heavy-based skillet or frying pan and sauté the onion until it is transparent, about 4–5 minutes.

Stir in the cabbage, apples, sugar and salt. Cover and cook on low heat for about 10–15 minutes.

Stir in the wine, vinegar and redcurrant jelly. Cover and continue to simmer on low heat for about 30 minutes until cooked. Drain and serve hot, as an acompaniment to your favourite savoury dish.

Sauerkraut

Contrary to what most people think, sauerkraut did not originate in Germany. It came apparently from China, and Ghenghis Khan is credited with introducing this pickled cabbage to Europe. The vitamin C properties of cabbage were first discovered by an English doctor in the 1700s when he noticed that Dutch soldiers did not get scurvy, which is caused by vitamin C deficiency. Their secret? They ate lots of sauerkraut. It became official: the cheap and versatile humble cabbage was also good for you. This

---

Apple Strudel

APFELSTRÜDEL

SERVES 6–8

This is one of the few occasions I will suggest using a ready-made pastry, especially phyllo or filo pastry. Life is too short to spend hours making something you can easily purchase at the supermarket, and the commercial varieties are excellent.

125 g/4 oz breadcrumbs

1 kg/2 lb cooking apples

juice of 3 lemons

250 g/8 oz cranberries (fresh or tinned)

250 g/8 oz seedless raisins

2 teaspoons ground cinnamon

1/2 teaspoon freshly grated nutmeg

250 g/8 oz coarsely chopped walnuts or pecans

180 g/6 oz soft brown sugar

500 g/1 lb packet of frozen phyllo (filo) pastry sheets, thawed

180 g/6 oz butter or margarine, melted

To serve:

ground cinnamon, nutmeg and caster

sugar, mixed together

fresh cream (optional)

Heat up a dry skillet or frying pan on medium heat, then pour in the breadcrumbs. Stirring all the time, lightly toast the crumbs for about 1–2 minutes. Remove from the heat and set aside to cool.

Peel, core and dice the apples, put them in a large bowl and cover them with the lemon juice. Add the cranberries, raisins, cinnamon, nutmeg, walnuts or pecans and the sugar. Mix well together.

Now comes the tricky bit. You will need four very moist tea towels. Spread two of them separately on a work surface and place the thawed sheets of pastry on one of them. Carefully lift off one sheet of pastry and place it on top of the second tea towel. Quickly cover the remaining pastry sheets with the third tea towel.

Brush the single pastry sheet with some of the melted butter or margarine and sprinkle with some breadcrumbs. Uncover the pastry sheets, lift off another sheet of pastry and place this on top of the first. Cover the remaining sheets as before.

Brush the second sheet of pastry with butter or margarine and sprinkle with breadcrumbs. Repeat this procedure with another two pastry sheets. On the fourth sheet, leaving about 2.5 cm/1 inch margin around the left, bottom and right of the pastry layers, spread half the apple and walnut filling. Take it up to about one-third of the way towards the middle of the sheet.

Using the tea towel underneath, slowly and carefully roll the sheets of pastry forwards to form a log, hiding the filling and all the while tucking the edges inwards as you go. Keep going until your strudel log is fully rolled.

Lightly grease a baking tray and carefully place the strudel log on it. Cover with the fourth tea towel until ready for baking.
Repeat the whole exercise with remaining pastry sheets and apple filling to make a second strudel log.

Preheat the oven to 180°C/350°F/Gas 4.

Brush the tops of both logs with the remaining butter or margarine and bake in the oven for 30–40 minutes until brown and crisp. Remove from the oven and allow to cool a little, about 20 minutes. Serve the strudel sprinkled with the spiced sugar mixture, either by itself or with fresh cream.

Shoofly Pie

SERVES 4–6

This is sometimes called Wet Bottom Cake because it has just that, a moist bottom. It is a popular local dessert in Pennsylvania. Make it according to personal taste, with a drier bottom if you prefer, but the one thing all shoofly pies have in common is the molasses, which tends to attract flies. So be ready to shoo the flies from your pie. This is how it got its name.

For the base:

250 ml/8 fl oz molasses

80 ml/2½ fl oz hot water

one 22.5 cm/9 inch uncooked pie shell
whipped cream or vanilla ice cream, to serve (optional)

For the topping:

250 g/8 oz plain flour

125 g/4 oz brown sugar

125 g/4 oz butter or margarine

½ teaspoon baking powder

½ teaspoon ground cinnamon

Pre-heat the oven to 190°C/375°F/Gas 5.

Stir the molasses and hot water together. Set aside.

In a large mixing bowl, combine all the topping ingredients and rub them together until the mixture resembles breadcrumbs.

Pour the molasses mixture into the pie shell and sprinkle the topping evenly over it. Bake in the oven for 45 minutes. Serve warm to hot, with whipped cream or vanilla ice cream if you wish.

Funnel Cake

DRECHTER KUCHA

SERVES 16–20

This cake gets its name from how it is made: thick pancake batter is put into a funnel, swirled out into a vat of hot oil and fried into a flat round mass. It is sprinkled with icing sugar and eaten as it is, or topped with a fruit or plain syrup. Funnel Cake is popular in the Midwest, and at lots of fairs around the country.

1 litre/2 pints milk

3 eggs

3 teaspoons baking powder

750 g/1 ½ lb plain flour

vegetable oil for frying

icing sugar or syrup, to serve

Beat together the milk, eggs and baking powder in a large bowl. Continue beating as you add small portions of sifted flour until a thick but flowing consistency is achieved (a cross between thick pancake batter and a muffin mix). It should be thick and creamy, but runny enough to pass through a funnel or large nozzle of a piping bag. If too thick, it will not flow; if too thin, it will flow too fast. Adjust the consistency by adding either more flour or more milk.

Heat up some oil in a heavy-based skillet or frying pan. Check the temperature by dipping a fork coated with batter into the hot oil. If it sizzles, the oil is ready for frying.

Starting from the middle and using a coiling motion, pipe out a steady stream of batter into the hot oil. Cook and brown one side, then turn over and cook the other side. When both sides are cooked and golden, remove from the oil and drain on paper towels. Serve immediately, sprinkled with icing sugar or topped with plain or fruit syrup.

Cheesecake

SCHMIERKUCHEN OR SMEARKUCHEN

SERVES 3–4

This cheesecake of Bohemian origin is very popular in New Ulm, Minnesota. The difference between European German cooking and New Ulm German American cooking is that in New Ulm desserts are generally sweeter. European Germans use more bitter chocolate and their cream isn't automatically sweetened.

500 g/1 lb prunes, stoned

sugar to sweeten prunes, if necessary

1/2 teaspoon freshly grated nutmeg

2 teaspoons ground cinnamon

3 teaspoons dried yeast

180 ml/6 fl oz warm water

750 g/1 1/2 lb plain flour

30 g/1 oz butter or margarine

30 g/1 oz caster sugar

30 g/1 oz butter, melted

375–500 g/12–16 oz cottage cheese or Philadelphia cream cheese

fresh cream, to serve

Pre-heat the oven to 180°C/350°F/Gas 4.

Put the prunes in a small amount of water and cook them until they are tender. Discard any excess water and mash up the prunes. Taste and adjust the sweetness by adding sugar if necessary, then stir in the nutmeg and half the cinnamon.

Put the yeast in a small container and add the warm water. Stir until dissolved, then let stand as you prepare the topping.

Put the flour, butter or margarine and the sugar in a bowl and rub together until the mixture resembles breadcrumbs. Add the yeast and mix together to form a dough. Cover well and put in a warm place to rise for about 30–40 minutes.

Sprinkle flour on a pastry board. Using a rolling pin, roll out the dough to a flat round of about 22.5 cm/9 inches in diameter and 1 cm/1/2 inch thick. Grease a 22.5 cm/9 inch pie plate with some butter, sprinkle with a little flour and swirl the plate around so the surface is evenly covered in flour. Shake off the excess.

Place the flattened dough in the pie plate, cover well and leave to prove in a warm place. It should double in size.

Brush all around the edges of the dough with some of the melted butter. Mix 2 tablespoons melted butter with the cheese. Press the dough down and spread the cheese evenly over it, then dot the prunes all over the top and smooth down. Sprinkle with the remaining cinnamon and bake in the oven for about 45 minutes or until cooked and golden brown. Serve hot, with cream.

Iced Coffee

EISKAFFEE

SERVES 4–6

6 cups of extra-strong freshly brewed coffee

6 scoops of vanilla ice cream

300 ml/¹/₂ pint whipped cream

a mixture of dark chocolate shavings and I teaspoon instant coffee powder

Let the freshly brewed coffee stand until cooled. Place I scoop of vanilla ice cream in the base of 6 tall sundae glasses. Fill each glass two-thirds full with coffee, then top with whipped cream. Finally, sprinkle with the coffee and chocolate mix. Serve immediately, with long spoons.

Fruit Punch

BOWLE

SERVES I5

This makes a refreshing drink in hot weather, so it is always a hit with summer guests. You can use any fruit of your choice according to the season, what's available and how much. It is best prepared a few hours in advance.

8 ripe pieces of either unpeeled apricots or peeled peaches, or I kg/2 lb strawberries or ripe pineapple, diced

125 g/4 oz caster sugar

250 ml/8 fl oz dry sherry

4 x 750 ml bottles of riesling

crushed ice

Put your chosen fruits into a huge container, sprinkle with the sugar and drizzle the sherry over the top. Cover and leave to stand for 4–6 hours.

Stir in the wine, add crushed ice and serve immediately.

Italian American **Tastes**

Safatia Romeo shows me her stuffed lobsters in Gloucester, Massachusetts

Almost since the first Italian stepped onto American soil, Italian food has been a huge success. Right across the States, Italian chefs have transformed people's eating habits. Popular items on the menu of the cheap and homely "spaghetti joints" that sprang up every-where were pizza, pasta, ice-cream and Chianti. In those early years of assimilation, Italian immigrants aspired to become American, while Americans began their long love affair with eating Italian. The cuisine that emerged was Italo-American. Like the early immigrant Chinese chefs, Italian restaurateurs were eager to please the clientele's bland palate, sweet tooth and passion for meat, along with their different ways of serving up courses and dishes. For example, meat and pasta began to be served together, meats appeared in traditional vegetable dishes, and salads were served before, instead of after, the main course – all quite unknown in Italy. Gradually Americans learned to overcome their nervousness of garlic, olive oil and strong-tasting cheeses. They travelled to

Fishing boats in the port of Gloucester, Massachusetts

Europe, enjoyed the varied delights of regional Italian cooking, and went home fired with enthusiasm for authentic Italian cuisine. Happily, Italian and Sicilian immigrants have continued to arrive, especially after the Second World War, bringing with them the knowledge and experience of Italian ingredients and cooking still fresh in their minds and mouths.

Immigrants from Italy first began to arrive in the New World in the mid-nineteenth century. They were recruited and brought to America as labourers to build railways, and to work on construction sites as carpenters, bricklayers and plasterers. Stitchmakers and dressmakers came to work in the clothing and shoe factories. Some of the best tailors came from Italy and their influence dominated fashion in the US garment trade. Many Italian women created now famous confectionery businesses. They began by working for low wages, struggling to raise their large families in cramped conditions in tightly packed tenements alongside Jewish, Polish and Irish immigrants. Italians settled in New York, Boston, Chicago, Philadelphia and San Francisco. In every city they created their own "Little Italy" with their churches, social clubs, restaurants, grocery stores and community pride and spirit. No doubt there were tensions in these overcrowded multi-ethnic urban communities of large families from very different backgrounds and cultures struggling to make ends meet, but on the whole they co-existed and even tried to support each

other in the worst times. Their languages, religions and eating habits were very different, but perhaps it was because they were all trying to be Americans at the same time that they were less aware of their differences. The success of these close-knit communities was strongly influenced by religion, traditional family values, respect for law and order, and a desire to give their children a strict upbringing and a good education.

In California, the rich vineyards were largely cultivated by Italian farmers, while fishermen from Italy and Sicily, along with the Irish and Portuguese, moved to both the Pacific West Coast and the Atlantic East Coast and formed the bulk of the fishing fleets there. The first generation of immigrant fishermen were a brave and hardy people who worked very hard to save enough money to buy their own fishing boats. Whole families owned a boat, while sometimes also running a food or grocery store. When a boat sank or was lost in the dangerous Atlantic waters, many members of one family often perished with it. Fish was not especially popular in the early years although it was plentiful and cheap, so it was a struggle to make a living. The only time they made a decent living was during Lent, Christmas and Easter, when the Catholics ate more fish. The majority of young fishermen left their boats to fight in the Second World War, and the fleets were seriously depleted. After the war, the huge Russian and Scandinavian fish factory ships moved in,

Nunzio is making fresh ricotta cheese at Purity Cheese in the North-End of Boston

The joys of lobster fishing with Jay Gastafero in the waters of Gloucester, Massachusetts

and only a few small fleets now work the coastal waters.

Whereas many immigrant communities gradually dispersed as times improved, many Italian communities have remained, mainly because they have established a flourishing trade in imported Italian foods, as well as popular restaurants, bakeries and Italian cafés, where office workers and shoppers come to eat and buy specialities and delicacies which they take home and cook into their own home-made "Italian" meals. Markets, delicatessens and grocery stores are filled with freshly made pasta, and Italian cheeses like mozzarella, Parmesan, ricotta, gorgonzola and pecorino are either imported or made on the premises by traditional methods. The bakeries sell warm, fresh-baked loaves of Italian breads, and the *pasticcerie* display a lavish array of trays of cakes, biscuits and cassata. Here you can find hard almond *biscotti* for dunking in sweet pudding wines, and soft-centred marzipan cakes, so delicious eaten with cappuccino. Italian delicatessens are filled with olives, numerous varieties of virgin olive oil, fresh herbs, cans of tomatoes and anchovies, and packets of polenta, borlotti and lentils. There is salami, pepperoni and prosciutto, Italian vegetables such as broccoli, artichokes, courgettes, aubergines and garlic,

and citrus fruits, peaches and melons.

The Depression in the 1930s brought terrible hardships. Many clothing and shoe factories, furniture stores, pool rooms, restaurants and fish markets were forced to close, causing massive job losses in the Italian communities. Many families were forced onto welfare for food and fuel, but the communities stuck together and tried to support each other. Fishermen shared out the unsaleable fish from their catch. Crabs found entangled in the nets were steamed and sold from a pushcart, hot pizzas and Italian breads and pastries were sold by peddlars on the streets. People still had to eat and Italians knew better than most how to create cheap, nourishing and delicious meals with poor cuts of meat, fresh vegetables and herbs grown in their backyards. They made them into endless dishes of pasta and rice that stretched the ingredients and filled the stomachs of the largest families.

Everyone knows that Italians are warm and hospitable. I discovered that in America, too, it is impossible to go into an Italian-American home without being offered some delicious food and a glass of good wine. Either side of the Atlantic, nothing has changed.

Cioppino

SERVES 6–8

Cioppino is a famous fish dish, which originated in a restaurant on Fisherman's Wharf in San Francisco. By "taste of mouth", the reputation of this recipe has spread throughout the United States, and now the original dish and its variations can be found everywhere – even including the little fishing port of Gloucester near Boston.

1 large onion, peeled and finely chopped

1 medium green pepper (capsicum), de-seeded and finely chopped

2 celery sticks, finely sliced

1 large carrot, cleaned and finely chopped

3 garlic cloves, peeled and finely minced

3 tablespoons olive oil

500 g/1 lb can Italian peeled tomatoes

250 ml/8 fl oz puréed tomatoes/passata

1 tablespoon coarsely chopped fresh basil leaves

1 bay leaf

1 teaspoon salt

1/2 teaspoon freshly ground black pepper

500 g/1 lb swordfish or halibut steak

1 dozen fresh mussels or clams in their shells

375 ml/12 fl oz dry white wine

250 g/8 oz fresh raw prawns, shelled and de-veined

250 g/8 oz fresh scallops

3 tablespoons finely chopped fresh parsley, to garnish

Combine the onion, pepper, celery, carrot, garlic and olive oil in a heavy-based saucepan or casserole dish and sauté the vegetables on medium heat for about 15–20 minutes. Stir in the tomatoes, tomato purée, basil, bay leaf, salt and pepper. Increase the heat and bring to a rolling boil for a minute or two, then reduce the heat to low and simmer for about 2 hours.

In the meantime, skin and wash the fish and cut it into bite-size pieces. Scrub the mussels or clams thoroughly.

Stir the white wine into the sauce and remove and discard the bay leaf. Add the swordfish, prawns and scallops, cover and simmer for 10 minutes. Arrange the mussels or clams in a layer on top of the fish in the saucepan. Cover and steam for about 10 minutes or until the shells are fully opened and the swordfish flakes easily. Discard any shellfish which does not open in the cooking.

Ladle the cioppino into serving bowls and sprinkle with parsley to garnish. Serve hot, with crusty Italian bread.

New England Clam Chowder

SERVES 2

Italo-American communities in the fishing port of Gloucester are seriously into fish, so I guess their love of clams stands to reason. They use them in stuffing, soups and in other imaginative ways.

2 tablespoons vegetable oil or butter

3 rashers of lean bacon, diced

1 medium onion, peeled and finely chopped

500 ml/16 fl oz milk

1 large peeled, raw potato, diced

600 ml/1 pint water

1/2 teaspoon salt

10 fresh clams in their shells, thoroughly cleaned

Heat the oil in a saucepan and brown the bacon. Remove the bacon from the oil and set aside. Sauté the chopped onion in the oil for about 3–4 minutes on medium heat. Add half the milk, all the potatoes, the water and salt, then lower the heat and boil until the potatoes are cooked and soft, about 10 minutes.

Add the remaining milk and the clams. Cover and cook for another 5–10 minutes until the clams are cooked and the shells open. Discard any unopened clams. Sprinkle the bacon on each helping and serve hot.

Fish Chowder

SERVES 4–6

In Gloucester, fish chowders come in many forms. This is an easy one I picked up.

500 ml/16 fl oz water

1 medium onion, peeled and finely chopped

1 kg/2 lb potatoes, washed and diced

1/2 teaspoon salt

1 kg/2 lb haddock or other similar fish

180 g/6 oz butter or margarine

salt and pepper

2 teaspoons cornflour, blended with 1 tablespoon fresh milk

170 g/180 ml can evaporated milk

750 ml/1 1/4 pints fresh milk

1/2 teaspoon paprika

Put the water, onion, potatoes and salt in a saucepan and bring to a boil. Lower the heat to medium and cook the potatoes until they are almost done, about 10 minutes. Add the fish and cook for a further 10 minutes or until both the potatoes and fish are well cooked. Once the fish flakes easily, add the butter, salt and pepper, the blended cornflour and the two types of milk. Heat through without boiling, stirring all the time. Sprinkle with the paprika and allow the chowder to stand for about 15 minutes until it sets. Serve warm.

Stuffed Breast of Chicken

SERVES 4–6

While filming around Boston's North End recently, I saw lots of evidence of southern Italian heritage deliciously expressed in the cooking and warm atmosphere. I was also able to sample equally mouthwatering northern Italian cuisine, such as in this chicken dish that cleverly combines three main ingredients I like, chicken, cheese and spinach.

6 large chicken breasts, beaten flat with a meat mallet

For the stuffing:

750 g/1½ lb fresh spinach (leaves only), washed and coarsely chopped

90 ml/3 fl oz extra virgin olive oil

1 onion, peeled and finely chopped

2 garlic cloves, peeled and finely chopped

250 g/8 oz fontina cheese, grated

½ teaspoon freshly grated nutmeg

½ teaspoon salt

For the wine sauce:

45 g/1½ oz butter

30 g/1 oz plain flour

180 ml/6 fl oz chicken stock

125 ml/4 fl oz dry white wine

juice of ¼ lemon

salt to taste

Make the stuffing: bring some water to a boil in the bottom part of a steamer and quickly steam the spinach in the top part until wilted, about 4–5 minutes. Remove the spinach, place in a sieve and press out the excess moisture with a wooden spoon. Set aside.

Heat one-third of the olive oil in a heavy-based saucepan and sauté the onion and garlic until they turn golden. Add the spinach, lower the heat and continue to sauté for about 3-4 minutes. Remove from the heat and set aside for about 5 minutes before you add the cheese, nutmeg and salt. Stir to mix well.

Pre-heat the oven to 110°C/225°F/Gas ¼.

Place the flattened chicken breasts on a chopping board, place equal amounts of the spinach mixture in the middle of each one and fold each firmly into a roll. Secure with wooden cocktail sticks.

Heat the remaining olive oil in a skillet or frying pan and lightly brown the outsides of the stuffed chicken, about 5–10 minutes. Remove from the oil and arrange in a heatproof serving dish. Place in the oven to keep warm.

Make the wine sauce: drain off the oil from the pan and wipe the pan clean. Melt the butter in the pan on low to medium heat, then blend in the flour with a whisk for about 1–2 minutes to make a quick roux. Carefully blend the chicken stock and wine into the roux to form a smooth sauce. Cook for about 2 minutes, then remove from heat, add the lemon juice and season to taste. Retrieve the chicken from the oven and pour the sauce over the top to totally cover the chicken. Serve immediately, with hot steamed rice and a crisp green salad.

Veal Parmigiana

SERVES 4–6

I learnt something today. Maria told me that Veal Parmigiana is an American dish, there is no such thing in authentic Italian cuisine. Maria Barker Pace is the owner of Nicole's Restaurant in Boston's North End. Maria has an excellent reputation as a health-conscious cook. I went to find out how she does it, so she cooked this lovely meal for me and my film crew. Maria showed us the sort of hospitality that reminded us that Italy was very alive and kicking, right in the heart of Boston. She was warm, generous and gracious, and she cooked like there was no tomorrow.

125 ml/4 fl oz olive oil, for frying

6 lean veal steaks (about 125 g/4 oz each), beaten flat with a meat mallet

375 g/12 oz plain flour

3 large eggs, beaten with a pinch of salt

500 g/1 lb finely grated Parmesan cheese (halve this amount if you do not want a strong taste)

a sprig of fresh basil, to garnish

For the sauce:

125 ml/4 fl oz olive oil

1 medium onion, peeled and chopped

2 garlic cloves, peeled and finely chopped

500 ml/16 fl oz puréed peeled Italian tomatoes/passata

3 tablespoons chopped fresh basil

salt and pepper to season

First make the sauce: heat the oil in a large heavy-based skillet or frying pan and sauté the onion and garlic until lightly golden, about 5 minutes on medium to high heat. Add the tomatoes, basil and seasoning to taste, stirring regularly. Lower the heat and continue to simmer for about 15–20 minutes, stirring regularly, until the sauce has reduced in volume and thickened.

Pre-heat the oven to 110°C/225°F/Gas 4.

In a separate heavy-based skillet or frying pan, heat up the olive oil for frying. Coat one piece of veal at a time first with the flour, shaking off the excess, then with the beaten eggs, shaking off the excess, and finally with the Parmesan cheese, shaking off the excess. Gently place the coated veal steak in the hot oil to fry. Repeat this process with the other pieces of veal, cooking 2–3 pieces at a time according to the size of your pan. Cook first on one side until lightly golden, then turn over and cook the other side, about 3–4 minutes on each side. Remove from the heat and keep warm in the oven until all the veal is ready.

Arrange the veal on a serving platter, accompanied by freshly cooked pasta of your choice. Spoon the thick rich sauce over the top of both the pasta and veal so that it drapes beautifully. Sprinkle with the remaining grated Parmesan cheese, insert a sprig of fresh basil in the middle and serve hot.

Polenta with Quails

SERVES 4–6

Isn't it interesting how polenta is now enjoying a popularity surge? For years this yellow Italian cornmeal has had bad press as peasant food, a kind of "carbohydrate on legs" designed as a filler to make a little go a long way. These days, it is fashionable to serve polenta. The world has awakened to its versatility and embraced it as the new gourmet carbohydrate to accompany exotic culinary creations.

12 quails, drawn and cleaned

2 packets of sunflower shoots or alfalfa, to garnish

For the marinade (2 quails):

125 ml/4 fl oz olive oil

2 garlic cloves, peeled and finely chopped

3 teaspoons garlic salt

500 ml/16 fl oz Moselle or Lambrusco wine

60 ml/2 fl oz mushroom soy sauce

60 ml/2 fl oz soy sauce

3 tablespoons tomato sauce

For the polenta:

60 ml/2 fl oz olive oil

12 medium thin slices of polenta (below)

You can ask a specialist butcher to splay the quails for you, or do it yourself. To splay your own quails, wash the quails thoroughly under cold running water, then drain and pat dry with paper towels. Put each quail on a chopping board and cut vertically right through the breastbone using a pair of kitchen scissors. Spread the bird flat out face down on the chopping board and press down on the back bone to flatten it even more.

Mix together all the marinade ingredients and pour over the splayed quails in a large casserole dish. Make sure each bird is well coated with marinade. Cover and refrigerate overnight.

Pre-heat the oven to 180°C/350°F/Gas 4.

Grease a roasting tin and arrange the quails in it. Set the marinade aside for later. Roast the quails for about 20–30 minutes or until they are well cooked.

Meanwhile, heat a griddle until it is so hot that a drop of water sizzles when splashed onto it. Brush the griddle with the oil. Grill the polenta, first on one side and then on the other, about 1–2 minutes each side. When ready, cut each slice into 2 triangles and keep hot. Pour the marinade into a small saucepan and simmer on low heat to reduce the volume of the liquid by one-third, about 10–15 minutes. To serve: arrange 2 slices of polenta apex to apex like a butterfly on a warmed dinner plate. Arrange 2 quails on top, drizzle the marinade over everything and garnish with sunflower shoots. Repeat with remaining polenta, quails, marinade and shoots. Serve hot to warm.

Polenta

SERVES 4–8

1.5 litres /2½ pints water

1½ teaspoons fine salt

250 g/8 oz yellow cornmeal (polenta)

Pour the water into a heavy-based saucepan and bring it to a boil on high heat. Stir in the salt until dissolved. Lower the heat to medium and pour in the cornmeal, stirring all the time. Cook until the polenta is done and starts to leave the sides of the pan, about 15–20 minutes.

Quickly grease a chopping board and pour the hot polenta onto it. Allow to cool, then refrigerate – it firms up and keeps well when chilled. When needed, cut into slices or different shapes and fry or grill.

Fritto Misto di Pesce

SERVES 6–8

An old Italian favourite, *fritto misto* means "a mixed fry-up", and *di pesce* means "of fish". Everyone has an opinion on the best way to coat the fish before frying. Some people prefer just straight flour and seasoning, some add water and chopped parsley to the flour and seasoning to make a light batter, others substitute milk or beer for the water. The Italians we filmed in the Boston region are proud of their southern Italian roots, so can they offer any American variations on the theme? Oh yes, many!

500 g/1 lb each fresh baby squid with tentacles, calamari (squid) rings, raw prawns, whitebait and white fish (eg whiting)

For the seasoning:

1 tablespoon paprika

1 teaspoon turmeric

salt and freshly ground black pepper

finely chopped fresh parsley (optional)

1½ cups plain flour for coating

vegetable oil for deep-frying

To garnish:

3 lemons, cut into wedges, fresh parsley

Opposite: Fritto Misto di Pesce.
Following pages: Kofta with Tomato Sauce (p.95) and Chicken Soup with Kneidlach (pp.91–92).

Wash and clean all the seafood. Leave the tails on the prawns but remove and discard the rest of the shells. De-vein the prawns: cut down the line of the spine with a sharp knife just deep enough to expose the vein without cutting right through the prawn. Remove and discard this vein. Wash the prawns, pat them dry, then splay each one into a butterfly shape. Sometimes you can buy pre-prepared prawns at your fishmonger, but naturally they cost a little more.

Mix all the seasoning ingredients in a large bowl together with a generous amount of flour. Heat up some oil for deep-frying until very hot. Coat each piece of seafood well with the seasoning mix and shake off the excess. Deep-fry in small batches in the oil until cooked and golden crisp on the outside, 1–2 minutes according to size. Remove with a slotted spoon, drain on paper towels and keep hot in the oven while you cook the remaining batches. Garnish with lemon wedges and parsley. Serve hot, with a fresh green salad and bread.

Spaghetti alle Vongole

SPAGHETTI WITH CLAM SAUCE

SERVES 4–6

Red tomato pasta, green spinach pasta and speckled mushroom pasta are now a common sight in many a pasta shop, but most pasta purists would throw up their arms in despair at the thought of avocado or purple beetroot pasta. "What is the world coming to?" they'd say. On my travels around the North End of Boston, I found such varieties of fresh pasta that my eyes spun in their sockets! Italy has arrived, American style. How to choose, what to choose? What would you have, ma'am? I settled for the devil I knew, plain spaghetti alle vongole . . . to buy time to think. Even that sauce came in a variety, so I chose the white sauce for a change from the usual tomato. Afterwards I got to thinking, why not combine the two? So here is what I came up with.

1.5 kg/3 lb fresh clams in their shells (about 45–50 small clams)

125 ml/4 fl oz olive oil

3 garlic cloves, peeled and finely chopped

1 fresh red chilli, de-seeded and finely chopped

250 ml/8 fl oz dry white wine

1 tablespoon tomato purée

4 plump ripe tomatoes, blanched, de-seeded and finely diced

salt and pepper

500 g/1 lb thin spaghetti (assorted colours, either fresh or dried)

1 bunch of fresh parsley, finely chopped, to garnish

It saves time if you can buy ready-cleaned clams, but if not, soak the clams in salted water overnight or a few hours to rid them of sand. Rinse them vigorously under cold running water while you scrub any debris from their shells with a firm brush.

Place the clams in a large saucepan on medium heat, cover and allow to heat up for about 5 minutes until the shells open. Give the pan a couple of healthy shakes in between, to encourage the clams to open.

When all, or the majority, of the shells are open, remove the pan from the heat and leave the clams to sit until cool enough to handle, about 3–4 minutes. Discard any unopened clams. Drain off the collected clam juice into a bowl, then strain through fine muslin to trap any remaining sand.

Select a few attractive clams in their shells and set aside for garnish later. Using a short but reasonably sharp knife, remove the remaining clams from their shells, discard the shells and return the clams to their juice in the bowl.

Prepare the sauce: in a skillet or frying pan, heat the oil and fry the garlic and chilli on low heat for about 3 minutes or until the garlic is golden and the chilli soft. Mix half the wine with the tomato purée and add to the pan with the diced tomatoes. Season with salt and

Illustrated opposite.

lots of freshly ground black pepper. Stir and cook for about 1 minute, then add the remaining wine and all the clams – the ones in their juice and the ones set aside in their shells. Stir well and cook on medium heat for about 4 minutes. Turn off the heat, cover and allow to stand while you prepare the pasta.

Bring a lot of salted water to a boil in a large saucepan. Add the pasta and boil rapidly until al dente. Remove and drain, then toss everything together in a giant cooking pot and heat through.

Pour the pasta and sauce into a warmed huge serving dish, arranging the clams in their pretty shells around the top. Sprinkle liberally with the chopped parsley. Serve hot, with a side dish of bread for mopping up any residual sauce afterwards.

Catfish Pizzaiola

SERVES 6–8

There are so many fish which are underutilized, either because of their looks or because people do not know what to do with them. One such fish with bad press is the catfish. Sefatia Romeo, a feisty local character among the Gloucester fishermen's wives, treated me to this mouthwatering rendition during the annual celebrations for the Festival of St Peter, patron saint of fishermen. I now look at catfish with admiration.

**2 kg/4 lb catfish
(or any white fish like cod)**

125 ml/4 fl oz olive oil

For the seasoning:

750 g/1 1/2 lb dry breadcrumbs

4 tablespoons chopped fresh parsley

4 tablespoons grated Romano or Parmesan cheese

10 cloves of garlic, finely chopped

For the topping:

250 g/8 oz tomato purée

1 medium onion, sliced into thin rings

2 tablespoons dried oregano

4 tablespoons grated mozzarella cheese

Pre-heat the oven to 180°C/350°F/Gas 4. Grease a large baking dish.

Mix together all the ingredients for the seasoning in a large bowl.

Put the olive oil in a dish. Dip each piece of fish in the oil, tap off the excess oil, then dip the fish in the seasoned breadcrumbs to coat all over. Carefully arrange the crumbed fillets in the baking dish. Smear the top totally with the tomato purée and arrange half the onion rings on top.

Mix the remaining oil with the remaining seasoned breadcrumbs and sprinkle evenly over the top of the fish. Sprinkle the oregano on top as well, followed by the mozzarella cheese. Garnish with the remaining onion rings and bake in the oven for 40 minutes. Serve hot.

Baked Stuffed Lobster

SERVES 3–4

The fishing community have a saying in Gloucester, "The lobsters are big in Gloucester!" Everywhere I went, somebody or someone told me that. I dismissed it all, thinking they needed to say that to sell the town and its produce to outsiders like me. I was wrong. On the day of the Festival of Saint Peter, when everybody was chanting "Viva San Peeeedro" and dancing in the streets, I walked into Sefatia Romeo's mother's house full of festival revellers, acrobats, mascaraders, dancers and "greasy-pole" walkers. Somebody offered me the biggest stuffed lobster I have ever seen!

3–4 medium or large lobsters

60 ml/2 fl oz vegetable oil

I large onion, peeled and finely chopped

4 garlic cloves, peeled and very finely chopped

250 ml/8 fl oz tomato purée and water

125 ml/4 fl oz red wine

250 g/8 oz cooked canned clams with their juice

500 g/I lb dried breadcrumbs, or half breadcrumbs and half crumbled unsalted Ritz crackers

I ½ tablespoons dried oregano

I heaped teaspoon garlic salt

I tablespoon grated Parmesan cheese

I tablespoon finely chopped flat-leaf parsley

Get the fishmonger to partially cut each lobster in half vertically without separating the halves. At the same time, have the lobsters cleaned and the intestines discarded. The lobsters should be nice and fresh – grey brown. They turn orange once cooked.

Heat the oil and sauté the onion and garlic on medium heat until they are translucent, about 5 minutes. Add the tomato purée and water, cook for 3 minutes, then add the wine and the clams and their juice. Cook for another 5 minutes.

In a large mixing bowl, mix together the breadcrumbs (or breadcrumbs and Ritz crackers), oregano, garlic salt, Parmesan and parsley. Make a well in the middle and pour in the sauce. Stir and mix into a very soft dough. Cover and set aside.

Place each lobster on a chopping board and stuff carefully with the prepared mix, making sure the cavities are well filled. Do not overstuff. Push the halves together to encase the stuffing. Repeat the exercise with remaining lobsters and stuffing.

Lightly grease a baking tray. Arrange the lobsters, head-to-tail, on the tray. Bake in the oven for 45–60 minutes. Check halfway to ensure all is well. Serve with a crisp green salad.

Aghoitta alla Novello

STEW WITH FISH CROQUETTES

SERVES 4–6

Food and drinks were flowing freely on St Peter's Day in Gloucester. I arrived at Nina Lovello's house just after lunch, but there was no way she was going to let me get away without tasting her food . . . Nina is a seriously good cook and the president of the local fishermen's wives' club. She says her aim is always to cook fish at its best. She does, believe me. This is a good way to use up leftover bits of fish which are not big enough to use for anything else.

For the croquettes:

750 g/1 1/2 lb boneless white fish of your choice, minced or ground

250 g/8 oz breadcrumbs

60 g/2 oz Romano cheese, finely grated

2 garlic cloves, peeled and finely chopped

1 tablespoon chopped flat-leaf parsley

3 eggs, beaten well

1 teaspoon salt

1/2 teaspoon freshly ground black pepper

oil for frying

For the sauce:

3 tablespoons olive oil

125 g/4 oz onion, peeled and very finely chopped

375 ml/12 fl oz canned Italian peeled tomatoes, chopped

250 ml/8 fl oz water

extra salt and pepper to taste

4 medium potatoes, peeled and quartered

250 ml/8 fl oz water or white wine (optional extra)

Make the croquettes: in a large mixing bowl, combine the fish with the breadcrumbs, cheese, garlic, parsley, eggs, salt and pepper. Mix very well together, then form into little sausage-shaped croquettes.

Heat some oil for frying in a heavy-based skillet or frying pan and fry the croquettes until golden brown on all sides. Remove from the heat, drain on paper towels and set aside.

Make the sauce: in a separate skillet or frying pan, heat up the olive oil and sauté the chopped onion on medium heat until soft, about 4 minutes. Add the tomatoes, water and salt and pepper to taste. Boil briefly for about 3–5 minutes. Add the potatoes and cook another 10 minutes before you add the croquettes. If necessary, add more water or white wine to cover the croquettes and cook for another 10 minutes or until the potatoes are done and the sauce reduced. Serve hot.

Codfish Balls or Cakes

SERVES 4–6

This is a quick recipe, which would be good as an appetizer, snack or light lunch, especially when eaten with sauce and salad.

3 medium potatoes

salt and pepper to taste

1 teaspoon butter

500 g/1 lb cod

250 g/8 oz dried breadcrumbs (home-made or bought)

4 tablespoons finely chopped flat-leaf parsley

2 tablespoons finely grated Parmesan cheese

2 garlic cloves, peeled and very finely chopped

2 large eggs

oil for deep-frying

Peel the potatoes and boil them in salted water for about 15-20 minutes. Drain and mash with the butter; set aside.

Boil the cod in salted water on medium heat until it flakes easily, about 10–15 minutes. Drain and flake the fish into a mixing bowl. Add the remaining ingredients, including the potatoes. Mix thoroughly. Form into little round pattie cakes, about 5 mm x 1 cm/¼ x ½ inch, or into small balls the size of table tennis balls.

Heat some oil in a deep heavy-based skillet or frying pan and deep-fry the fish balls until golden brown all over. Remove from the oil and drain on paper towels. Serve hot, with or without sauce (see below).

Codfish Balls in Sauce

To turn the codfish balls into a more substantial meal, put 375 ml/12 fl oz canned peeled Italian tomatoes in a saucepan, add 250 ml/8 fl oz white wine and bring to a boil on medium heat. Peel and dice 2 medium potatoes and add to the pan. Add ½ teaspoon each salt and pepper and 1 small onion, peeled and finely chopped. Lower the heat and cook for about 10–15 minutes or until the potatoes are cooked. Add the fish balls and sprinkle 1 tablespoon finely chopped basil on top. Stir, increase the heat to medium and simmer until the sauce is reduced, about another 10 minutes. Serve hot, with a green salad and Italian bread.

Zabaglione

SERVES 4

Apparently, *zabaglione* means "eggnog". I don't know about you, but I love Italian food so much that I often glut on it so that by the end of the meal I have no room left to enjoy the many "crave-able" Italian desserts. That is why I tend to choose light desserts, like water ices and the odd zabaglione.

250 g/8 oz assorted berries

3 tablespoons caster sugar

4 egg yolks

125 ml/4 fl oz Marsala

Take 4 long-stemmed glasses or parfait glasses, divide the berries among them and chill the glasses.

Whisk the sugar and eggs together in a medium mixing bowl set over a saucepan of boiling water. Whisk until well blended, creamy thick and looking like lemon curd. This should take about 2–3 minutes.

Lower the heat and remove the mixing bowl from the pan. Add a little cold water to the boiling water in the pan to quickly reduce the boiling temperature to simmering. Return the mixing bowl to its original position and continue to whisk the egg and sugar mixture for about another 3 minutes.

Add the Marsala and continue to whisk as the zabaglione takes shape, becomes frothy with air and the volume increases. Carefully spoon the zabaglione into the chilled glasses on top of the berries. Serve immediately.

Savoiardi Delight

SERVES 6–8

This is an old favourite of mine, which I couldn't resist sharing with you because the last time I made it was at Ketteridge Farm just outside Boston, where we stayed during the Boston shoot. It was very hot and the house was not air-conditioned. We had long days of shooting and by end of day, everybody suffered. The crew was restless. I decided on an age-old remedy for discontent – food, preferably sweet food. We were filming "Italian" weren't we, so why not my *Savoiardi* pudding? It worked, and the filming went well.

500 ml/16 fl oz fresh thick cream (for whipping)

250 ml/8 fl oz chocolate liqueur

250 ml/8 fl oz Bailey's Irish Cream

250 g/8 oz caster sugar

500 g/1 lb Savoiardi (Italian sponge biscuits)

300 g/10 oz very dark or bittersweet chocolate, grated

In a blender, combine the cream, the chocolate liqueur, the Bailey's and the sugar. Blend well.

Arrange a layer of one-half of the biscuits evenly along the bottom of a large and deep dessert container or casserole dish. Pour one-half of the blended cream and liqueurs evenly over the biscuits. Sprinkle one-half of the grated chocolate all over the top. Press the biscuits down after each application to make sure they absorb the liquid.

Arrange the remaining biscuits in another layer on top, then pour the remaining cream mixture over them and sprinkle with the remaining chocolate. Put in the refrigerator and chill for 12–24 hours until set. Slice and lift portions out when ready. Serve cold.

Melon Shake

SERVES 1–2

Melon shakes are so easy and so refreshing in hot weather that I guess it was inevitable this drink would be popular in health-conscious America.

1 large ripe ogen melon

Chill the melon in the refrigerator overnight for best results. Peel the melon and cut the flesh into strips. Using a juicer, juice the melon pieces. Melon juice comes out thick and creamy with a big head of froth on top, just like a milk shake but without the calories. Do not add sugar. Pour into parfait glasses and serve immediately.

Jewish American **Tastes**

Rabbetzin Esther Winner and her children admiring their Sabbath table of goodwill and love

It is difficult to think of Jewish food without also thinking of Jewish festivals, the Jewish faith and the Jewish people. The quartet is inseparable. Food, for the Jewish people, is intricately bound up with their religion and identity. The history of Jewish cuisine is the history of the Jewish people, because Jewish cooking is literally an act of faith, whose roots are to be found in the traditional religious feasts and holidays. Jews have always been unwitting cultural nomads. Consequently, Jewish food has become as peripatetic as the people.

There are now more Jews living in New York than in any other part of the world – even Israel. Millions of Jews have travelled to America in search of safety and freedom. So it is not surprising that the Jewish American story is a rich tapestry of hundreds of years of Jewish history and culture brought to the United States from all corners of Europe, North Africa and the Middle East. The Ashkenazi Jews, the largest group, come from Europe, especially the Central and Eastern areas. The Sephardi Jews originate from Spain, North Africa and the Middle East. Numerous Jews and non-Jews now enjoy Jewish-style food, such as bagels, cheesecake, gefilte fish, latkes,

My first pastrami sandwich at the famous Katz's deli in the Lower East Side of New York

matzahs and pastrami, eaten in busy and often famous delicatessens. Many of these familiar-sounding foods originate in the cultures in which Jews have previously lived. For example, Sephardi Jews eat felafel, kofta, hummus and other Arab and Iberian traditional food. Similarly, Jews whose families came from Russia, Poland, Bavaria and Romania have incorporated dishes from those regions into their own cultural cuisines and made them "Jewish".

The Jewish American cuisine today is genuinely cosmopolitan. As they moved and settled among different cultures, they adopted a wide variety of dishes. Jewish food is not just Polish, Russian, Syrian or Arabic, it is unique and different because it has become a part of the Jewish experience. But Jewish food is not truly Jewish unless it is kosher.

Jewish cookery is based on strict dietary observances known as kosher. The laws which govern kosher are known as Kashrut. Keeping kosher is an intrinsic part of the daily life of an observant Jew. An expert would need a book to explain all the details, but, briefly, there are three categories of kosher foods: meat, dairy and parev. One of the main rules is the total separation of meat and dairy products. They may not be cooked together as a dish nor as separate dishes at the same meal. In fact, one should wait several hours after eating one before eating the other. To ensure this rule is kept, the kosher kitchen

contains separate sets of cookware, dishes and preparation areas for meat and dairy. The third group, parev, is made up of foods that are neither meat nor dairy and can be eaten with either. Vegetables, fruits, eggs, fish and grains are examples of parev foods. There are also certain foods that are trefa, forbidden. Consumption of animal blood is not permitted, and meat must be slaughtered and prepared according to kosher regulations. Only animals that both chew their cud and have split hooves may be eaten: cows, sheep and goats, for example. Pigs, camels and hares are forbidden. Kosher fowl include chickens, ducks, geese and turkey, but not birds of prey or scavengers. Fish, a parev food, may only be eaten if it has both fins and scales. Cod, haddock, herring, snapper and salmon have these. All shellfish, eels, octopus and shark, are non-kosher.

The keeping of kosher is central to the belief that the Jewish faith is everywhere in daily life – in the kitchen and at the table. The mother who keeps a kosher kitchen and feeds her family kosher meals is ensuring the Jewish values of present and future generations. This may feel familiar to many of us who have travelled far from other cultures and faiths. In the modern Jewish American home, the degree of observance of kosher is a strong sign of how close they still feel to their roots. In New York, at least, there is a growing movement of Jews returning to the

Quality control – inspecting freshly-baked matzahs at the matzah factory in New York

kosher kitchen or, at least, to the Jewish table, to celebrate the feasts that mark their identity.

A very small group of Sephardi Jews first arrived in New York as early as 1654. This community was further swelled by vast numbers of Ashkenazi Jews from Eastern Europe, escaping the pogroms in their homelands as well as grinding poverty. Many settled in the Lower East Side in the 1830s and 1840s, where they became peddlers and merchants. The third and largest wave of immigrants came between 1887 and 1924. Religious Jews from Russia, their numbers now a staggering one and a half million people, mostly squeezed into the ever-expanding Lower East Side of New York. Families who were originally farmers and lived off the land were crammed into tenements and became the urban poor. They brought with them their diet, which was a peasant "poor food". They made potato latkes, bagels, matzah ball soup, one pot meals like cholent, and foods they could carry with them in their daily work, such as knishes, pirozhki and burekas. It was hard to get fresh food, so they pickled the vegetables and salted the meat and fish. The now-famous pastrami is a Rumanian word for beef that has been pickled and smoked. The keeping of kosher food preparation was often lost in the desperate daily battle to feed themselves, but as the New York communities or shtetlachs (shtetls) established themselves and prospered, people started to re-introduce kosher laws and religious observances, such as keeping the Sabbath and celebrating Hanukkah and Passover.

So why is Jewish food still so important to Jewish Americans, whether they are from the strict Chassidic communities, are practising Orthodox, Conservative, Reform, Assimilated or in some way still regard themselves as Jewish, but do not practise all the Jewish rituals and laws? Fifty per cent of Jewish New Yorkers are totally assimilated in modern American life, do not attend synagogue or observe Sabbath, do not eat kosher and have married non-Jewish partners. But almost all these Jews will tell you that they are Jewish and still eat traditional Jewish meals, particularly when celebrating a Jewish holiday among their family. For the other half for whom religion, heritage and cultural identity is of overriding importance, keeping kosher and religious observance in every part of their daily life is a priority. It provides a symbolic focus to the days of the week that has remained unchanged over the centuries.

Apart from a few ritual dishes, such as cholent, challah and matzo, it is not the food itself that counts, but whether it has been prepared according to kosher regulations, and whether it is eaten together with other Jews. The Jews are generous and hospitable; they also have a sentimental attachment to home cooking, and to those dishes cooked by the Jewish immigrant mother who turned meagre ingredients into nourishing heartwarming meals for her family.

The pastrami production line at Katz's

Chicken Soup

SERVES 6–8

This version of chicken soup was given to me by Rebbetzin Esther Winner. I met Esther at Brighton Beach, Brooklyn, New York, where she and husband Rabbi Winner live with their children, surrounded by a community of mainly Russian and other Jews, Rabbi Winner's congregation. Esther looked beautiful and radiant . . . she was expecting another baby. We chatted animatedly as I watched her make matzah balls for her chicken soup, salmon stuffed with gefilte fish and finally finish her Shabbat preparations with a touching lighting of the candles with her children. With Esther's permission, I bring you her chicken soup and her salmon, with a few additions of my own purely as a matter of individual preference.

3 litres/6 pints water

1 whole boiling chicken, cut into 6–8 pieces (ask your butcher to do this for you)

salt and pepper to taste

2 medium onions, peeled and quartered

2 parsnips, peeled and quartered

3 carrots, peeled and quartered

2 courgettes, peeled and quartered

2 celery sticks including leaves, cut into 4 long strips each

4 garlic cloves, peeled and left whole

1 leek, cut into thirds

2 red chillies (optional)

2 celeriac, quartered (optional)

Kneidlach or Kreplach (below)

For the bouquet garni:

1 bunch each of fresh parsley, dill and coriander

1 bunch of fresh basil (optional)

1 bunch of fresh thyme (optional)

a couple of strips of lemon peel (optional)

Make the bouquet garni: clean all the herbs and leave them intact. Put them with the lemon peel (if using) in a piece of cheesecloth and tie together well.

Pour the water into a large stock pot, add the chicken pieces and salt and pepper and bring to a boil. Allow to boil for about 15 minutes, then lower the heat and skim off any residue from the top of the water. Add all of the vegetables and the bouquet garni. Bring to a boil again and simmer on medium to low heat for 2-2½ hours until the chicken is well cooked.

Skim off most of the oil that has collected on top of the soup, but leave a little behind for authenticity (see below). Remove the bouquet garni, vegetables and chicken pieces. Save the chicken pieces. Discard the bouquet garni and vegetables, or save the vegetables and mash them with separately boiled potatoes and some non-dairy margarine.

For a nice clear broth, pour the soup through a fine sieve. Return to the pot, re-heat and keep warm. The soup can be served as it is, or with either Kneidlach or Kreplach. It could also be served with noodles, rice, mashed potatoes and vegetables, challah bread or a combination of any of these according to individual preference. Serve hot, when everything is ready.

Kneidlach

MATZAH BALLS

MAKES ABOUT 24

Kneidlach is derived from the German word for dumpling, *Knödel*. Putting dumplings in soup to increase its volume and spread the cost of feeding many is quite common in many peasant and poor cultures around the world. However, this style of serving soup became Jewish because it was also a staple in the home countries of many Eastern European or Ashkanazi Jews. To make it even more special at Passover, many Jews started to use kosher matzah bread or matzah flour to make their dumplings. Some prefer to buy ready-prepared, kosher matzah flour, while others, the purists, prefer to buy matzah bread and make their own flour.

2 large matzah breads or 125 g/4 oz matzah flour

2 large eggs, yolks and whites separated and yolks checked for the presence of blood

salt to taste

about 2 litres/4 pints water

Chicken Soup

Chicken soup would have to be the one meal most people automatically refer to as Jewish food. From its role as a panacea for every ailment to that of a Jewish mother's act of love for her family, the simple chicken soup has come a long way to enjoy its elevated status. It is even referred to on occasions as "the Jewish penicillin". There are so many variations on the theme of chicken soup, or the "goldene yoich" as it is also called because of the golden globules of oil which collect from the chicken and stay afloat on top of the finished soup. These days, for health reasons, this oil is often skimmed off and discarded before serving.

If using matzah bread instead of pre-prepared flour, break the bread into small pieces by hand into a food processor. Cover and grind on high for 10–20 seconds, or until the bread is reduced to flour. If not, repeat the action until it is.

Lightly beat the egg yolks until frothy. Set aside. Whisk the egg whites until stiff. Gently fold the egg mixtures together and slowly fold in the matzah flour until well mixed. Cover and chill in the refrigerator for about 30 minutes.

Bring the water to a boil in a large saucepan or casserole dish and season with a little salt. The balls expand during cooking, so make sure you have enough water. Using clean hands, shape portions of the matzah mixture into small balls about 2 cm/1 inch in diameter and drop carefully into the boiling water. Continue until all the mixture is used up. Lower the heat and simmer for about 30 minutes. Drain off the water and add to the soup before serving.

Cholent

SERVES 6–8

This classic slow-cooking stew is made with beans, meat, marrow bones – and many other things. It is generally eaten on the Jewish Sabbath, hence it is usually made during the day on Friday and left to cook slowly for 8–12 hours so that it is ready for lunch on Saturday Sabbath after returning from prayers at the synagogue. This recipe is a mixture of all the various cholents I have eaten, from Egypt and Morocco to Australia and the United States.

125 g/4 oz each chick peas, red kidney beans, butter beans, haricot beans and black-eyed peas (beans)

3 small onions, peeled and quartered

4 garlic cloves, peeled and 2 left whole, 2 finely chopped

125 ml/4 fl oz corn or other vegetable oil

8 small potatoes, peeled

125 g/4 oz barley or burgul

250 g/8 oz brown rice

1 tablespoon salt

2 teaspoons pepper

1 teaspoon turmeric

a large pinch of saffron (threads)

1 teaspoon paprika

1 teaspoon ground cumin

1/2 teaspoon ground cinnamon

500 g/1 lb chuck steak or brisket, cubed

500 g/1 lb lamb shanks, cut into small pieces

3 small marrow bones or veal shin bones

125 g/4 oz dried apricots

125 g/4oz prunes

2 litres/4 pints water

Cholent Kneidlach (below)

8 eggs, in their shells

1 medium bunch of fresh coriander, chopped

Soak all the beans together in cold water overnight, then rinse and drain. Clean out any stones and discoloured beans. Pour the beans into a large casserole dish which has a tight-fitting lid. Add the onions, the whole garlic and the oil and sauté for about 5–10 minutes.

Pre-heat the oven to 180°C/350°F/Gas 4.

Add the potatoes to the bean mixture and sprinkle the barley or wheat and the rice on top. Add half the salt and the water and bring to a boil. Lower the heat and continue to boil for about 20 minutes, skimming off the scum as it rises to the surface.

Mix together the salt, pepper and spices and dredge the meat chunks through it. Arrange all the meat and bones on top of the bean mixture and sprinkle with remaining garlic and spices.

Arrange the apricots and prunes on top, cover with foil and cook in the middle of the oven for about 30 minutes. Remove from the oven, make a small well in the middle and place the kneidlach dumpling in the well. Carefully arrange the eggs around the dumpling and in amongst the meat and vegetables. Sprinkle the top with the coriander and add more water if necessary. Cover with the foil and the lid to fully seal in the food. Return to the oven, reduce the heat to 110°C/225°F/Gas 1/4 and continue cooking for 8–12 hours. Serve warm, unveiling the stew at the table so everyone can share its fantastic aroma. Serve each guest a slice of dumpling and an egg with their stew.

Cholent Kneidlach

CHOLENT DUMPLING

Sometimes this is also called Cholent Kugel.

90 g/3 oz margarine

375 g/12 oz plain flour or matzah flour

1 egg

1 teaspoon tomato purée

1 tablespoon finely chopped fresh basil or parsley

a pinch of salt

½ teaspoon each paprika and turmeric

Rub the margarine into the flour until it looks like breadcrumbs. Add the remaining ingredients, mix well together and knead into a dough. If necessary, add more flour or water to make the dough soft and pliable. Form into a round dumpling and place in the middle of the cholent before the final leg of the cooking, as in the recipe above.

Cholent

Cholent goes by many names, depending on whether you are an Ashkenazi or Sephardi Jew. Even then, there are still variations therein. For instance, *cholent* or *chulent*, the Eastern European Ashkenazi Jewish words, are thought to have come from the French word *chaud*, meaning warm, while *hameen*, one of the many Sephardi Jewish words for the same stew, takes its origins from the Hebrew word *ham*, meaning hot.

Cholent can be prepared on top of the cooker, in which case you will need to place a heat diffuser or thin sheet of metal under the pan, over low heat. The heat diffuses through the metal and foods keep cooking and stay warm without getting too hot. By using this method, Jewish cooks can observe Sabbath laws and not have to light the cooker on the Sabbath.

Kofta

MAKES ABOUT 30, TO SERVE 4–6

Kofta, boulettes, yullikas and albondigas are all common names for meat balls in the Mediterranean and the Middle East. The spices and ingredients change according to the country you are in. This recipe is Sephardi Jewish in style, a mixture of all the above.

1 litre/2 pints water seasoned with 1 teaspoon salt

1 kg/2 lb lean minced beef

1 medium onion, peeled and very finely chopped

2 garlic cloves, peeled and very finely chopped

2 tablespoons cornflour, matzah flour or breadcrumbs

180 g/6 oz chickpea flour

60–90 g/2–3 oz rice of your choice, boiled

1/2 teaspoon cayenne pepper

1/2 teaspoon paprika

1/2 teaspoon ground cumin

1/2 teaspoon ground cinnamon

2 teaspoons salt

2 large eggs

1 tablespoon tomato purée

1 tablespoon very finely chopped fresh thyme

For the Tomato Sauce

12 over-ripe tomatoes

8 tablespoons finely chopped fresh basil

salt and pepper to taste

Bring the seasoned water to a boil. Meanwhile, combine all the ingredients in a large bowl and mix well. Wet your hands and form the mixture into small balls about the size of table tennis balls. Drop the meat balls carefully into the boiling water. Lower the heat and cook on medium to low heat for about 35–40 minutes. Serve warm to hot, with Tomato Sauce.

Tomato Sauce

For the tomato sauce: Put the tomatoes in a bowl and pour boiling water over them to cover fully. Allow to stand for about 10 minutes. Using a slotted spoon, remove the tomatoes one by one and peel off the skin. Blend the tomatoes with the basil and seasoning to taste. Serve hot or cold.

Knishes or Burekas

MAKES 24 GOOD-SIZE KNISHES

Knishes are well-known and popular Ashkenazi savoury pastries, often filled with minced beef, potato, cheese, cabbage or other vegetables, or a combination of any of these. The name is thought to have been corrupted from a Slavic cake roll called knysz. The beauty of knishes is that they can be made small and served as finger food or formed into a large roll for family dinners. These days some people find it easier to use frozen pastry rather than make their own.

For the pastry:

2 teaspoons lemon juice or cider vinegar

I teaspoon salt

60–90 ml/2–3 fl oz ice-cold water

625 g/20 oz plain flour

60 ml/2 fl oz corn or other vegetable oil

125 g/4 oz butter or margarine

I egg, lightly beaten with 125 ml/4 fl oz milk for glazing

For the filling:

90 ml/3 fl oz half vegetable oil and half margarine

2 large onions, peeled and finely chopped

2 garlic cloves, peeled and finely chopped

3–4 large potatoes, boiled in their skins and still hot

2 large eggs, lightly beaten and seasoned with salt and lots of freshly ground black pepper

125 g/4 oz each grated Parmesan and crumbled feta cheese (optional)

Make the pastry: mix together the lemon juice or vinegar, salt and water. Sift the flour into a mixing bowl and make a well in the centre. Pour the oil into the well, add the butter or margarine and rub together with your fingertips until the mixture resemble breadcrumbs.

Slowly add the lemon juice mixture to the flour, a little at a time. Gently knead together as you do this until you eventually have a smooth, malleable dough. Add more flour or water if necessary.

Place the dough on a floured board and knead well with the heel of your hand for about 2–3 minutes. Form the dough into a ball, put it back in the bowl and cover well to prevent it drying out. Leave in a cool place for 20–30 minutes until ready to use. The dough freezes well, so you can make a big batch if you like, and save the extra dough for another time.

Make the filling: heat the oil and margarine in a heavy-based skillet or frying pan, add the onions and garlic and fry until brown on medium to low heat, about 10–15 minutes. Peel the potatoes, cube them, then stir them into the onion mixture. Cook on medium heat for 5 minutes, stirring regularly. Add the beaten eggs and stir well to mix, then cook for about 3 minutes. Remove from the heat and mash everything together, with the Parmesan and feta if you like. Allow to cool until needed. Taste and adjust seasoning.

Pre-heat the oven to 180°C/350°F/Gas 4.

Using a floured rolling pin, roll out the dough on a floured board until it is thin, about 3 mm/⅛ inch thick. Cut into 7 cm/3 inch rounds or squares. Place 1 tablespoonful of the filling in the middle of each piece of pastry and bring the edges together, either upwards or folded over. Pinch the edges firmly together to seal, then brush with the egg and milk mixture.

Arrange the knishes on a greased baking tray and bake in the oven for about 30–40 minutes or until browned. Serve hot or warm, as you wish.

Home-made Chicken Liver Pâté

SERVES 4–6

It is almost impossible to write about Jewish American recipes and not mention liver of some sort because liver is such an integral part of the food repertoire of the Jewish American. In traditional recipes, schmaltz (rendered chicken fat) is used for frying, but I prefer the flavour of oil. This pâté can be served as an appetizer or entrée.

125 ml/4 fl oz vegetable oil

3 large onions, peeled and finely chopped

4 large garlic cloves, peeled and finely chopped

500 g/1 lb chicken livers

2 bay leaves

salt and pepper to taste

125 ml/4 fl oz medium sweet sherry (optional)

additional bay leaves and dry biscuits, to garnish

Heat up the oil and sauté half the onions and garlic until transparent, about 5 minutes. Add the livers, the remaining onions and garlic, the bay leaves and salt and pepper. Continue to cook on medium heat until all the water has evaporated and the livers are brown and cooked through. Drain off the excess oil and reserve. If using sherry, add it now, and stir for about 1 minute.

Remove from the heat, discard the bay leaves, then blend the liver mixture in a food processor or blender until almost smooth. Scoop out into a nice dish or mould, stir in the reserved oil and garnish with bay leaves. Refrigerate for about 3-4 hours, or overnight. Serve with dry biscuits.

Potato Latkes

SERVES 4–6

Potato latkes are Ashkenazi Jewish potato pancakes. There are many latkes one can make, but this potato one is the most popular. Latkes, pronounced "latkas" are usually served with the main meal at the Jewish Festival of Hanukkah, but they can be eaten any time. Yet another of my favourites.

5–6 large potatoes (1 kg/2 lb), peeled and cut into chunks

1 large onion, peeled and cut into chunks

3 large eggs, lightly beaten with a fork

125 g/4 oz plain flour or matzah meal

1–1 ½ teaspoons salt

½ teaspoon pepper

vegetable oil for frying

Using a cheese grater or food processor, coarsely grate the potatoes and onion together. Put in a sieve and press down to get rid of excess water. Pour the vegetables into a large mixing bowl and add the eggs, flour or matzah meal, salt and pepper. Stir and mix well to form a batter.

Heat up the oil in a heavy-based frying pan or skillet. Fry spoonfuls of the latkes at a time until all is used up (there should be about 24). Allow about 4–5 minutes before you turn them over to cook the other side. Cook until golden brown, taking care not to overcook. The idea is for the latkes to be soft and moist on the inside and brown and crunchy on the outside.

When cooked, remove from the oil and drain on paper towels. Serve hot or warm, as part of a main meal. Or serve them by themselves with tomato or apple sauce or other fruit or vegetable sauces as entrées or snacks.

Variation

You can substitute sweet potatoes, courgettes, carrots, parsnips and other vegetables for the potatoes, and you can also add some chillies, spices, curry powder, chopped curry leaves or cheese as an interesting change. Or you can mix a number of these together like I do sometimes.

Salmon à la Sea Breeze

SERVES 6–8

This is a salmon marinated and then stuffed with home-made gefilte fish before it is garnished and baked. It smells and tastes sensational. When I asked Esther, or shall I say Rebbetzin, Winner what she planned to call this recipe of hers, she gave me the name above. She said it's because she lives at Sea Breeze Avenue and this is a fish dish. Even more importantly, it is prepared using a fish with scales, a significant factor in the ruling of the Jewish faith. I watched Esther expertly show me how she does it, and I tried it too, in my kitchen back home. It was easy, so here it is, with her kind permission.

3 kg/6 lb whole salmon

2 tablespoons salt

1 tablespoon garlic powder

1/4 teaspoon black pepper

For the marinade:

5 garlic cloves, peeled and quartered

1/2 bunch of fresh coriander

1 large ripe tomato, quartered

2 tablespoons corn or other vegetable oil

2 tablespoons water

1/2 teaspoon table salt

1/4 teaspoon freshly ground black pepper

Gefilte Fish (see p. 100)

1 medium onion, peeled and sliced into rings

2 carrots, cut into small cubes

2 celery sticks, sliced into small pieces

1 large tomato, diced

250g/8oz can tomato juice or sauce (kosher)

5 garlic cloves, peeled and finely chopped

1 tablespoon lemon juice

1/2 teaspoon black pepper

1 teaspoon salt

125 ml/4 fl oz water

Ask your fishmonger to thoroughly clean the salmon and to scale, gut and bone it. Ask him to leave the head on, but remove the backbone so that the fish will open like a book. Prepare the fish by seasoning it inside and outside with the salt, garlic powder and black pepper.

Make the marinade: combine all the ingredients in a food processor and blend well for about 1 minute. Spread the marinade all over the fish, making sure you cover the inside and outside well. Cover with foil and leave to marinate in the refrigerator overnight, or for a few hours.

When ready to cook, pre-heat the oven to 180°C/350°F/Gas 4.

Grease a large deep baking dish.

Open out the salmon and fill the inside with the gefilte fish mixture. Close and place in the dish. Arrange the vegetables around the fish. Combine the tomato sauce and the remaining ingredients and pour all over the salmon and vegetables. Cover again and bake in the oven for 45 minutes to 1 hour.

Gefilte Fish

1.5 kg/3 lb minced or ground fish
(1 kg/2 lb white fish and 500 g/1 lb
pike or similar)

4 medium onions, very
finely chopped

60 g/2 oz matzah flour or plain flour

4 eggs, lightly beaten with a fork

1 teaspoon black pepper

5 teaspoons salt

about 4 teaspoons sugar, to taste

Mix all the ingredients together on medium speed in the mixing bowl of a bread mixer, or on low speed in a food processor, until well combined. Use as a stuffing for a whole fish as in the recipe above, or form into a log, wrap in greased foil and bake as a fish loaf. Alternatively, form into small balls and cook in hot seasoned fish or chicken broth and serve with Tomato Sauce (page 95).

Savoury Potato Kugel

SERVES 4–6

I've yet to come across anybody who does not like kugels, Jewish or goy. The beauty of kugels is that they are so versatile – you can add vegetables and or meat to your potato or noodle kugels, and you can also make sweet kugels, although they are not as popular as the savoury ones.

5–6 large potatoes (1 kg/2 lb), peeled and cubed, or half sweet potatoes and half plain potatoes

1 large onion, peeled and finely chopped

3 spring onions, topped, tailed and finely chopped

125 ml/4 fl oz vegetable oil

4 large eggs

2 tablespoons chopped fresh basil

2 tablespoons chopped fresh flat-leaf parsley

1–1 ½ teaspoons salt

1 teaspoon freshly ground black pepper, or to taste

Put the potatoes and onions in a large bowl and cover with cold water. Allow to soak for about 30 minutes, then drain.

Pre-heat the oven to 230°C/450°F/Gas 8. Grease 2 medium-size non-stick sandwich cake tins or, if preferred, a large non-stick roasting tin or baking dish with straight sides. Place in the middle of the pre-heated oven for about 10 minutes while you prepare the kugel mixture.

Combine all the ingredients in a food processor or blender and blend thoroughly into a smooth mixture. Remove the hot tin(s) or dish from the oven and pour in the mixture evenly. It sizzles invitingly as the mixture hits the base of the dish. After pouring, smooth over the top and place in the oven for 30 minutes. Reduce the heat to 180°C/350°F/Gas 4 and bake for a further 30 minutes. Turn off the oven and allow the kugel to breathe for about 10–15 minutes before serving. It can be served hot or cold by itself, or preferably as an accompaniment to a stew or roast, or a meat or fish dish of your choice.

Variations

This dish is particularly delicious when it is built up a little, so I suggest you add another layer to the existing one by repeating the whole process with another lot of ingredients. Once blended, just pour the second mixture directly on top of the first that is already baking in the oven. Continue cooking as per instructions and times until fully cooked and ready to eat.

Sometimes I add grated parmesan cheese to the ingredients in the blender and blend it in together. But a note of caution, should you add cheese to your potato kugel, you must not serve it with a meat dish if you intend it to remain kosher.

Pickled Herring and Potato Salad

SERVES 4–6

I love fish, yet I've never liked herring since I was little. I think this is a combination of having been made to sit for hours removing tiny bones from smoked herring so my mother could use the fish in her okra stew, and the fact that I generally dislike fish with many bones. Well, all that negative feeling disappeared the day I walked into Russ and Daughters, the fishmongers in New York. Mark Russ and his wife Maria dispelled any pre-conceived ideas I had with sample upon sample of herring fare – smoked herring, schmaltzy herring, pickled herring, herring salad – all without a trace of bones. I tried them all and I was converted.

500 g/1 lb pickled herring fillets

1 kg/2 lb diced boiled potatoes, peeled or unpeeled

250 g/8 oz celery with tops, finely sliced into thin crescents

4 spring onions with tops, finely chopped

1 handful parsley, cleaned and finely chopped

125 g/4 oz sour cream

1 ½ tablespoons fresh lemon juice

2 teaspoons sugar (optional)

Soak the herring in cold water for 10 minutes, then rinse and pat dry with paper towels. Cut the fillets into smaller strips. Combine the remaining ingredients together, mix well then stir in the herring fillets. Cover and leave for 3–4 hours, or even overnight, so the flavours of the ingredients can permeate one another.

Cheesecake

SERVES 8–10

"As American as cheesecake", I've often heard said, but I wonder how many who say it know that we have the American Jews to thank for this luscious dessert? According to Claudia Roden, in "The Book of Jewish Food", the humble cheesecake is a speciality of Shavuot – a Jewish festival for celebrating the giving of the Torah to Moses on Mount Sinai. As the Jews travelled around the world they took their beloved cheesecake with them. The current variations and toppings of fruit, cream, chocolate and toffee are probably more modern and American.

For the base:

1 packet (375 g/12 oz) sweet digestive biscuits or sweet whole-wheat biscuits, crushed to coarse powder in a food processor

60 g/2 oz brown sugar

1 teaspoon ground cinnamon

125 g/4 oz butter, warmed and melted

For the filling:

375 g/12 oz cream cheese

375 g/12 oz sour cream

250 g/8 oz sugar

1 teaspoon finely grated lemon zest

90 ml/3 fl oz fresh lemon Juice

1 teaspoon vanilla extract

a pinch of salt

3 eggs

Make the base: in a large mixing bowl, mix together the crushed biscuits, sugar, cinnamon and melted butter. When fully mixed, spread over the base of a 22.5 cm/9 inch springform cake tin and press down firmly and evenly. Place in the refrigerator to set, until ready to use.

Pre-heat the oven to 180°C/350°F/Gas 4.

Using a hand beater and a mixing bowl, or a food processor, beat together the cream cheese and sour cream until smooth and even. Add the sugar and beat a few seconds more, then add the lemon zest and juice, the vanilla and salt. Continue to beat as you add the eggs, one at a time. Beat only until all the eggs are blended, then stop. Do not overbeat or the cheesecake will crack more easily.

Pour the filling into the chilled base and bake for about 1 hour or until lightly browned on top and firm, both in the middle and around the edges. Turn off the oven and allow the cake to sit in the oven for 20–30 minutes before removing. Leave to cool down completely before serving.

The cheesecake can be served plain, or garnished as you wish. For a decorative topping, whip 250 ml/8 fl oz cream until firm, then pipe it on top of the cool cheesecake and decorate with either grated chocolate or slices of fresh or canned fruit. For a baked soured cream topping, see following page.

It is easier to cut cheesecake with a hot knife, so dip your palette knife or cake slice in boiling water each time before cutting your cake.

Sour Cream Topping

250 ml/8 fl oz sour cream

1 tablespoon caster sugar

1 teaspoon finely grated lemon zest

Beat all the ingredients together until blended. Spread over the top of the cool cake. Re-heat the oven to 200°C/400°F/Gas 6. Return the cake to the oven and bake for 5 minutes until the topping sets. Remove from the oven. Cool and chill until ready to serve.

Sweet Noodle Kugel

MILCHIK LOCHSHEN

SERVES —6

Like most tasty well-tried recipes, this one has been handed down from generation to generation in Arlene Agus's family. It is a favourite noodle dessert of her grandmother Bube. Arlene is a slim, stylish New Yorker with a zest for life. We met at a book launch she'd arranged and we took an instant liking to one another. The food at the function was tasty and trendy. We met over food and we parted with the promise of food – Arlene pressed this recipe in my hand for publication and I promised her dinner in England or Australia. Thanks Arlene and grandma Bube.

250 g/8 oz fine noodles

6 eggs

500 ml/16 fl oz milk

250 ml/8 fl oz sour cream

250 g/8 oz sugar

250 g/8 oz cream cheese

1 teaspoon vanilla extract

180 g/6 oz melted butter

500 g/1 lb cottage cheese

500 g/1 lb Cheddar cheese, grated

1 tablespoon ground cinnamon mixed with sugar to taste

Cook the noodles in boiling salted water for 8–10 minutes until soft and cooked. Drain in a colander and rinse under the hot tap.

Pre-heat the oven to 180°C/350°F/Gas 4.

Put the remaining ingredients, except the cinnamon and sugar, in a mixing bowl. Add 1 teaspoon salt and mix well together, then add the noodles and stir well to mix. Pour into a lightly greased 3 litre/3 quart casserole dish and sprinkle with the cinnamon and sugar. Bake in the oven for 1–1½ hours until light brown on top. Serve hot.

Honey Cake

SERVES 8–10

This Ashkenazi Jewish sweet cake is usually eaten at Rosh Hashanah, the New Year, as a symbol of how sweet or good the incoming year is expected to be. It is a fitting dessert to serve following Tsimmes, the sweet and sour stew also served at Rosh Hashanah. Like ginger cake and tsimmes, honey cake also dates back to medieval Germany. It is a good way to start any new venture if you are hoping for good luck.

250 ml/8 fl oz honey, warmed to make runny if not

4 large eggs

180 g/6 oz caster sugar

180 g/6 oz butter, melted

250 ml/8 fl oz strong black coffee, preferably made with freshly ground coffee beans

2 teaspoons baking powder

1 kg/2 lb plain flour

1 teaspoon bicarbonate of soda

1 teaspoon ground cinnamon

1 teaspoon ground allspice

Pre-heat the oven to 160°C/325°F/Gas 3. Grease a 30 cm/12 inch cake tin.

Whisk together the honey and eggs for about 3 minutes, then add the sugar. Continue to whisk for another minute before you add the butter and the coffee mixed with the baking powder. Whisk to mix, then add the flour, bicarbonate of soda, cinnamon and allspice. Whisk until well mixed. Pour into the greased tin and bake in the oven for about 1 hour until cooked and browned on top. Allow to stand in the tin to cool before turning out onto a wire rack.

> Honey has always played an important symbolic role in Jewish cooking. The symbolism can be traced back to the biblical reference, when God promised to deliver the Jews to a land of milk and honey.

Maple Syrup Chiffon Cake

SERVES 8–10

500 g/1 lb plain flour

180 g/6 oz caster sugar

180 g /6 oz dark brown sugar

1 rounded tablespoon baking powder

4 tablespoons maple syrup, warmed to make runny

125 ml/4 fl oz water

125 ml/4 fl oz corn oil

8 eggs, yolks and whites separated

250 g/8 oz pecans, finely ground

Pre-heat the oven to 180°C/350°F/Gas 4. Grease a 25 cm/10 inch cake tin.

Sift the dry ingredients into a large mixing bowl. Make a well in the middle and pour in the maple syrup, water, oil and egg yolks. Beat until fluffy, then fold in the ground pecans. Beat the egg whites until peaks form, then carefully fold into the cake mixture.

Pour into the tin and bake in the middle of the oven for about 1 hour or until the cake springs back when lightly pressed. Turn off the oven and leave the cake inside to cool totally, about 3–4 hours. Loosen the edges with a palette knife before inverting the cake to remove it.

Jewish Drinks

Observant Jews are generally very strict with their drinks, especially those containing grapes. These have stringent rules and regulations attached to their preparation. The whole process from beginning to end must be handled entirely by Jewish hands, particularly if the seal of the container is broken or opened. In my search for American Jewish drinks, I came across a number of sweet drinks, especially the home-made variety.

Raisin Syrup

ENOUGH FOR 6–8 DRINKS

This is a Sephardi Jewish drink.

1 kg /2 lb dark raisins

3 litres/6 pints water

3 tablespoons fresh lemon juice

Steep the raisins in the water for 1 hour to soften them. Bring to a boil, lower the heat and simmer on low heat for about 2 hours. Allow to cool a little, about 1 hour.

Work the mixture in small batches in a blender. Strain the blended liquid through fine cheesecloth, add the lemon juice and pour into a clean pan. Simmer on low heat until the liquid is reduced and thickened, about 40 minutes. Cool and serve as you wish, by itself or added to chilled fizzy water.

Fizzy Chocolate Milkshake

SERVES 1

Apart from kosher wines, it would appear that Jews drink much the same as anybody else. Strict observants of Kashrut would insist on making sure the content of any drink does not include non-kosher material.

90 ml/3 fl oz milk

250 ml/8 fl oz soda water

60 ml/2 fl oz chocolate syrup

drop of vanilla extract

Combine all the ingredients and whisk them together.

Serve immediately.

New Mexican Tastes

The Santa Fé market is bursting with goodies

The cuisine that the indigenous Mexican Indians and the Spanish colonists have together created over the centuries is now one of the most popular in the United States, and its culinary influence has spread throughout both South and North America.

The American Southwest region runs along the border with Mexico, and includes the states of Texas, New Mexico, Arizona and California. New Mexico is at the heart of the Southwest and the regional cuisine is often described as New Mexican, but in fact the cuisine as a whole is Southwestern. And Southwestern cuisine tastes good.

Much of the Southwest is a vast semi-arid landscape of mountains, high plains and desert that burns as hot as the chilli that famously grows there. The landscape would seem inhospitable to the newcomer, but the Indians who first lived there were well able to live off its hidden wealth. Long before the region was invaded by the Spanish and subsequently fought over and divided up between Mexico and the United States, the indigenous Indians were leading a settled and productive life, with a cuisine rich in variety and tastes.

The Aztecs in Mexico already enjoyed a diet of corn made into cornbread, corn tortillas and tamales, as well as beans, wild turkey, chocolate, fish, squash, cacti, tomatoes, avocados, the *piñon* (pine nut) and, of course, hundreds of different types and strengths of chilli. Further North, in what is now New Mexico and Arizona, the Pueblo people lived as village dwellers. They had long since learned to cultivate crops in harsh conditions with minimal rainfall, so it is not surprising that their religion and ceremonies are concentrated around rituals for fertility and rain. Later, the Navajo, a hunting people, came down from the North and lived alongside the Pueblo as farmers. As well as cultivating a wide range of vegetables, fruits and herbs, the Pueblo and Navajo also domesticated animals for food and hunted the abundant game. Later they became skilled herders of cattle and sheep brought to the region by the Spanish settlers.

When the Spanish originally landed on the shores of Mexico they were looking for gold. They found the gold, and another, more exciting, treasure – the chilli. Over the centuries, the Spanish settlers began exploring what is now the American Southwest. They found large quantities of silver and they also created vast ranches for their sheep and cattle. Catholic Spanish missionaries ventured North to convert the Native Americans and set up missions along the banks of the Rio Grande in New Mexico.

The Spanish food influence is central to modern

A cache of New Mexican spices at the Santa fé market

America. Spaniards brought their cows, sheep, goats and made their own traditional cheeses from their milk. They introduced the cultivation of wheat, grapes, citrus fruits and olives. They imported garlic, figs and dates, and spices such as cinnamon and cloves. Using local chillies and imported spices, the Spanish developed delicious, spicy hot sauces and marinades to baste their meats, fish and vegetables, which they cooked by barbecuing, a method they acquired from the indigenous Carib Indians on the various Caribbean islands. Racks of wooden sticks were laid over open fires to grill meat and fish, which the Caribs called *barbacoa*. Traditional New Mexican barbecues are still held at large family and community events, with huge cuts of meat cooked over open pits and then served with tortillas, beans and spicy salsas.

In New Mexico, as in all Southwestern states, chilli and corn are central to all cooking. Some of the finest chillies are grown here as well as many varieties of corn, in particular the blue corn. Southwestern food is always very colourful to look at, and there are many different colours of both chillies and corn, each slightly different and used in a variety of ways. New Mexico cuisine is a subtle mix of three cultures: Pueblo, Spanish and Anglo. It is said to be the most varied and unique, the most adaptable and most innovative. It is a far cry from the fashionable Tex-Mex, with its designer dishes such as chilli con carne. New Mexico is more remote and less populated than Texas

My first attempt at making tortilla, at Leona's kiosk outside El Santuario in Chimayo

or California. This has allowed the region to develop a style and distinctive flavours, as can be seen in dishes like carne adovada, tamales and blue corn enchiladas.

Whatever the regional differences in the Southwest, common to all is the tortilla, the staple "bread" still eaten by the people who trace their origins to pre-Columbian times. Made from the flour of ground dried corn mixed with lime and water, the tortilla is shaped and then baked on a hot stone or a modern hotplate. Tortillas are eaten with meat and vegetable dishes, often used instead of plate, knife or fork. For instance, fold over a corn tortilla, fry it into a crisp U-shape, fill it with any variety of seasoned meat, fish, beans and salsa and it becomes a taco; fill the tortilla with any selection of your choice, fry it until crisp all over and it becomes a tostada; fill up a tortilla, add salad and salsa, then roll it up into a sausage and wrap it in greaseproof paper and you have a burrito; dip a tortilla in oil, tomato or chilli sauce, fill it and douse it with green or red chilli sauce, then sprinkle it with grated cheese and bake it so it turns into an enchila-

da; stuff a tortilla, roll it into a pillow and fry it until it becomes a chimichanga. The list goes on . . .

The chilli, in all its many shapes, colours and flavours, is *the* essential ingredient for authentic Southwestern food. You can eat chillies fresh, dried, roasted, grilled, crushed, ground into a spice or whatever, it doesn't matter. What does matter, is that you eat them. Fresh chillies range in flavour or heat from mild to mouth burners: gentle, plump, sweet and fruity anchos; pungent, smoky, dark and alluring chipotles; aromatic and tempting bell peppers (capsicums); downright fiery, cheeky habañeros that could make you weep with pain or pleasure. The hotness is a matter of personal taste and stamina.

New Mexican cuisine makes no apologies – you either love it or hate it, but one thing is for sure, you can't ignore it. Whether you are a "chilli head" or just enjoy a dish of food full of flavour, colour and excitement, Southwestern cuisine is not just the hottest cuisine around, it is here to stay.

Con mucho gusto!

Tasting green chilli salsa with Cheryl Alters Jamison in her kitchen near Santa Fé

Cocido

SERVES 4–6

Soups are very popular in New Mexican and other indigenous cuisines, simply because they're a cheap and tasty way to make a little go a long way. This one is so full and filling it is almost like a stew. I bring it to you courtesy of Cheryl Alters Jamison and her husband Bill, passionate foodies like me, who live just outside Santa Fé, New Mexico. I have reduced the amounts a little for personal preference.

500 g/1 lb beef short ribs (spareribs)

1 litre/2 pints water

750 ml/1¼ pints beef stock

375 g/12 oz butternut squash or pumpkin, peeled and cubed

375 g/12 oz canned chick peas, rinsed and drained

¼ medium cabbage, finely shredded

1 large onion, peeled and finely chopped

1 medium potato, peeled and finely chopped

1 large carrot, cleaned and diced

45 g/1½ oz ground New Mexican red chilli pepper or paprika

3 garlic cloves, peeled and finely crushed

½ tablespoon salt

1 bay leaf

½ teaspoon dried thyme or 1 teaspoon chopped fresh thyme

125 g/4 oz chorizo sausage or any smoked and/or highly seasoned spicy sausage, thinly sliced

60 g/2 oz fresh coriander, finely chopped, to garnish

Put the ribs in a large stockpot or soup pot, add the water and bring to a boil. Reduce the heat to low and simmer for about 1 hour. Skim off any frothy sediment that collects on top of the water during this cooking process.

Add all the remaining ingredients to the pot, with the exception of the sausage and coriander. Cook for another 40 minutes or until all the vegetables are cooked and the meat is falling off the bones. Using a slotted spoon, carefully lift out all the meat and bones. Separate the meat from the bones, discard the bones and set the meat aside to cool.

Using a soup spoon, lift out half the vegetables with some soup stock and purée this in a blender or food processor. Return the puréed vegetables and stock to the pot. Add the meat from the ribs.

Lightly sauté the sliced sausage in a skillet or frying pan over low heat until crisp and brown. Add this to the soup and continue to simmer for a further 15 minutes. Serve warm to hot, garnished with the coriander.

Green Chilli Soup

SERVES 4–6

Chilli has been designated as New Mexico's state vegetable, as has the pinto bean. Too bad if you don't like either of these, but hopefully I can tempt you to fall in love with chilli once you have tasted this soup. As soon as you mention chilli, most people think only of the red burning variety. In New Mexico, the mellow and green, mildly hot chilli is the one most favoured, especially the locally grown New Mexican long green chilli with its distinctive flavour.

125 g/4 oz butter

2 medium red onions, peeled and very finely chopped

4 garlic cloves, peeled and very finely chopped

2 medium potatoes, peeled and diced

1 litre/2 pints chicken stock or broth

375 g/12 oz roasted and chopped mild green chillies (New Mexican green or Anaheim)

1 teaspoon dried Mexican oregano (mild and sweet)

1 teaspoon salt

125 ml/4 fl oz half milk half cream

125 g/4 oz Cheddar or Monterey Jack cheese, grated

a handful of chopped fresh coriander, to garnish (optional)

thin tortillas, toasted and cut into strips, to serve (optional)

Heat up the butter in a large stockpot or casserole dish and sauté the onions and garlic until the onions turn translucent, about 10 minutes. Add the potatoes and sauté for another 3 minutes before you add the stock, chillies, oregano and salt. Bring to a rolling boil. Lower the heat to medium and simmer for about 20–30 minutes or until the potatoes are cooked and soft.

Remove the soup from the heat and allow to cool for about 10 minutes before you purée the lot in small batches, using a blender or food processor. Return the soup to the cooking pot, add the milk and cream and heat well to warm right through.

To serve, place portions of grated cheese in each soup bowl, then ladle in the hot soup. Top with chopped coriander and serve with side helpings of warm tortilla strips (if using).

Not Many People Know That

On my filming trips and in my research, I amass a whole lot of largely useless information, but every so often I come across little gems like this: did you know that chillies were first cultivated as early as 4,000 BC by Indians from the highlands of the Andes, but that they were gathered for food much earlier – around 10,000 years ago? The word "chili" comes from the Mexican language of Nahuatl. In New Mexico, chile ends with an "e" when desciding the pod, but it is spelt chili with an "i" at the end when describing the dish. In the UK, both the pod and the dish are called chilli, and chillies is the plural of chilli. All very confusing.

Burritos with Potato and Bacon

SERVES 4

I've eaten many types and flavours of breakfast burritos and enchiladas, but I ate my first green chilli enchilada with local chorizo sausages served with hash brown potatoes at Hotel La Fonda in Santa Fé, New Mexico. It was so good, it had a spicy kick to get you started in the morning. I thought I was all set, until I tasted this burrito with bacon and potato, a speciality of Cheryl and Bill's.

60 ml/2 fl oz vegetable oil

I medium onion, peeled and very finely chopped

I garlic clove, peeled and very finely chopped

4 medium potatoes, parboiled, peeled and coarsely grated with a cheese grater

1/2 teaspoon salt

freshly ground black pepper

4 medium thick flour tortillas (18–20 cm/7–8 inches in diameter), kept warm in a low oven

8-12 lean rashers of grilled bacon, cooked according to personal taste

800 ml/1 1/2 pints Hatch Green Chilli Sauce (page 119), warmed

180-250 g/6-8 oz Cheddar cheese, grated

Pre-heat the oven to 200°C/400°F/Gas 6.

Heat the oil in a heavy-based skillet or frying pan and sauté the onion and garlic over high heat for about 2 minutes. Add the grated potatoes, salt and lots of freshly ground black pepper. Cook for 2–3 minutes. Press the mixture down into a firm pancake as you cook to ensure the heat penetrates right through to the middle. Carefully scrape the mixture up to turn it over and cook evenly. Each time, cook for about 2–3 minutes and turn again. Keep repeating the process until the potatoes are cooked through and have crisped and browned, about 10–15 minutes.

Spread out a warm tortilla and spoon a quarter portion of the potato mixture onto it. Top with 2–3 bacon rashers and roll loosely into a cylindrical shape. Place in a baking dish. Repeat the process with the remaining tortillas, potato mixture and bacon and arrange the burritos neatly inside the dish.

Pour green chilli sauce over the top, sprinkle with the cheese and bake in the oven for about 8–10 minutes or until cheese is melted and hot. Serve immediately.

Opposite: Elia's Chiles Rellenos (p.118).
Following pages: Succotash (p.135); Wild Duck with Cranberries and Wild Rice Stuffing (p.130).

Blue Corn Pancakes with Cider Syrup

SERVES 4–6

The American Southwest is considered the home of blue corn, originally from the Pueblo Indians of the region. Blue corn has become increasingly popular because of its original colour and nutty flavour – it adds an interesting dimension to cooking and presentation.

For the syrup:
60 ml/2 fl oz corn syrup
500 ml/16 fl oz cider
1 cinnamon stick
1 tablespoon butter

For the pancakes:
375 g/12 oz pine nuts
180 g/6 oz blue cornmeal
180 g/6 oz plain flour
1 teaspoon baking powder
2 tablespoons caster sugar
1/2 teaspoon salt
375 ml/12 fl oz milk
2 eggs
2 tablespoons melted butter
1/2 teaspoon almond extract
vegetable oil for frying

Heat up the corn syrup, cider and cinnamon stick in a heavy-based saucepan over medium heat and boil to reduce the volume of the liquid by about one-quarter. Turn off the heat and stir in the butter until it melts. Set aside.

In a food processor, first grind half the pine nuts. Once ground, add the cornmeal, flour, baking powder, sugar and salt. Process together for about 3–4 minutes. Pour the mixture into a large mixing bowl and add the milk, eggs, melted butter and almond extract. Beat well to mix thoroughly, cover and set aside in the refrigerator for about 30 minutes.

Preheat the oven to 110°C/225°F/Gas 1/4.

Heat a small amount of vegetable oil in a heavy-based skillet or frying pan and fry small portions of the pancake batter, allowing about 1–2 minutes before flipping them over to cook the other side for the same length of time. Add small amounts of oil as necessary. Continue until all the batter is cooked, keeping the pancakes warm in the oven until all the pancakes are done. Warm up the syrup and serve the pancakes hot, topped with the syrup and whole pine nuts.

Opposite: Elia's Sopaipillas (p.122).

New Mexican Carne Adovada

SERVES 4–6

This is a truly deliciously tempting meal, lean pieces of pork marinated and then cooked ever so slowly in a rich, thick red chilli sauce. It is usual to eat it with tortillas, but I actually prefer it with boiled rice and fiery hot chilli salsas. The choice is yours. I spent a very pleasant morning in the home of Cheryl Alters Jamison and husband Bill eating vast quantities of this stuff – I couldn't stop! New Mexican red chillies are recommended in this recipe, but the Chimayó variety of chilli peppers are best because of their size and wonderful balance of heat and sweet. If neither is readily available in your area, it is worth persisting to find them in a Mexican or other speciality shop.

1.5 kg/3 lb very lean pork, diced into 3.5 cm/1 ½inch cubes

2 teaspoons salt

250 g/8 oz New Mexican red chillies (about 25 whole dried chillies), stalks removed, de-seeded and rinsed

fresh salad greens and firm ripe tomatoes, diced, to garnish

For the sauce:

500 ml/16 fl oz chicken stock

1 medium onion, peeled and chopped

4 garlic cloves, peeled and finely chopped

2 teaspoons cider vinegar or sherry

3 teaspoons dried Mexican oregano

3 teaspoons ground coriander

Pre-heat the oven to 150°C/300°F/Gas 2.

Grease a large casserole dish, arrange the pork pieces in it and sprinkle with 1 teaspoon salt.

Arrange the wet chillies in single layers on baking trays and roast them in the oven for about 5–7 minutes, taking care not to burn them. Remove from the oven and allow to cool. Break each chilli into three pieces and divide into two lots. Some chillies may still be slightly moist, but that's okay.

Put one half of the chillies and half the stock together in a blender and purée. Repeat with remaining chillies, stock and the rest of the ingredients for the sauce. Pour all of this puréed sauce over the meat in the casserole dish, then sprinkle with the remaining salt. Cover and leave to marinate in the refrigerator overnight.

The next day, bring the adovada to room temperature before you bake it in the oven.

Pre-heat the oven to 150°C/300°F/Gas 2.

Bake the adovada for 3-3½ hours until the pork is well cooked and the sauce thickened and rich. Serve hot, garnished with salad and tomatoes.

Seafood Chimichangas

SERVES 4–6

Quite apart from being serious chilli eaters, New Mexicans eat a lot of meat and cheese. I know New Mexico is inland and has no sea, but I decided to grab the bull by the horns and substitute prawns for meat in a popular Southwestern recipe. Here is the result. Be fair, at least I've used New Mexican chilli sauce! You could also use chopped crab or lobster meat instead of the prawns.

3 tablespoons butter

1.5 kg/3 lb large raw prawns, shelled and de-veined or white fish, e.g. walleye or cod, deboned and finely chopped

125 g/4 oz spring onion tops, finely chopped

250 g/8 oz mushrooms, cleaned and finely chopped

3 garlic cloves, peeled and finely chopped

375 g/12 oz spinach, washed and thinly sliced

¹/₂ teaspoon salt

3 teaspoons lemon juice

6 thin tortillas (about 17.5 cm/7 inches in diameter)

vegetable oil for deep-frying

For the topping:

500 ml/16 fl oz warm Chimayó/Red Chilli Sauce (page 120)

250 g/8 oz Cheddar cheese, grated

Guacamole Sanchez Style (page 121)

250 ml/8 fl oz soured cream

250 g/8 oz firm ripe tomatoes, diced

Pre-heat the oven to 110°C/225°F/Gas ¹/₄.

Melt the butter in a heavy-based saucepan and sauté the prawns, spring onion tops, mushrooms, garlic, spinach, salt and lemon juice for about 7–10 minutes or until the prawns change colour to pink and the vegetables go limp.

Spread out the tortillas and divide the seafood mixture equally between them, spooning it over the middle of each one. Roll up each tortilla and tuck in the ends to form solid packages. Secure with wooden cocktail sticks.

Heat the oil in a deep heavy-based saucepan. Fry each chimichanga until golden, about 3 minutes, turning it over as it cooks to brown on all sides. Remove from the oil and drain on paper towels. Keep warm on a heatproof plate in the oven while frying the remaining chimichangas. Serve hot, topped with scoops of warm chilli sauce, cheese, guacamole, soured cream and diced tomatoes.

Natural Highs

I had hoped by combining seafood, thought for years to have similar aphrodisiac qualities to chillies, I'd have hit the jackpot of culinary stimulation with this dish. Alas, the only high you are likely to get is the wonderful taste, and possibly a "chilli high", thought to come from the messages our cells send to the brain after we eat chilli. The brain then produces morphine-like endorphins, giving us a natural high. Scientific studies apparently indicate that chilli is addictive. Real chilli lovers cannot get enough of it, so be warned . . .

Roque's Carnitas

SERVES 4–6

It was mid-June and hot, one of those hot Santa Fé days. So hot you got a headache just walking twenty minutes to the corner of Palace and Washington Streets to buy a carnita from Roque Garcia and his partner Mona Cavalli. Yet even that heat was not enough to stop people queueing at Roque's Carnita Cart. Roque has written on his cart, "*carne* means meat, *ita* means little, therefore carnita means little pieces of meat". In fact, Roque's carnitas are marinated strips of meat cooked with onions and seasoning, topped with Mona's salsa and served hot wrapped in warm tortillas. Roque is Mexican and learnt the recipe from his mum. I took my place in the queue and the sun . . .

1.25 kg/2¼ lb lean boneless sirloin steak, cut across the grain into thin julienne strips

2 tablespoons vegetable oil

6 thick flour tortillas (17.5–20 cm/7–8 inches in diameter)

For the marinade:

9 tablespoons vegetable oil

185 ml/6 fl oz soy sauce

3 tablespoons dried Mexican oregano or slightly less of other oregano

6 garlic cloves, peeled and finely chopped

For Mona's salsa:
2 firm and ripe medium tomatoes, finely diced

1 medium onion, peeled and very finely chopped

6 fresh jalapeños, finely chopped

3 tablespoons finely chopped fresh coriander

3 garlic cloves, peeled and finely chopped

The minimum preparation time for this meal is 24 hours, so start preparing it the day before cooking.

Put the strips of meat in a large stainless steel or similar non-reactive mixing bowl, mix all the marinade ingredients together and pour over the meat. Stir well to coat the meat thoroughly, cover and refrigerate for 12–24 hours.

In another large bowl, combine all the ingredients for the salsa and stir to mix. Cover and refrigerate.

When ready to cook, remove both the meat and the salsa from the refrigerator. Drain the meat and discard the marinade. Heat up the 2 tablespoons oil in a wok and gently swirl the wok so the oil coats the inside well. You need reasonably high heat for this. When the wok starts to smoke a little, sauté one-third of the drained meat for about 3–4 minutes, stirring constantly until cooked and lightly browned. Transfer the carnitas to a plate and keep warm while cooking the remainder. Start warming the tortillas.

Make the accompaniments (see overleaf): lower the heat under the wok and add the sliced onions and chillies, stirring all the time. Add mushroom soy sauce (if using) and cook for about 3 minutes.

Add the carnitas to the vegetables in the wok and toss them through to mix. Spread out a warm tortilla and, with a pair of tongs, lift out a

For the accompaniments:

2 medium onions, peeled and thinly sliced

7 mild green fresh chillies (prefer- ably New Mexican or Anaheim), sliced into very thin rounds

mushroom soy (optional)

lemon quarters

portion of carnita mix and fill the tortilla. Quickly roll into a sausage, leaving one open end for the salsa. Wrap first with foil to conserve the heat, then a large paper napkin to contain any spillage. Serve immediately, with lemon quarters, and topped with Mona's salsa.

Green Chilli Enchiladas

SERVES 4–6

Enchiladas are lightly fried corn tortillas wrapped around chicken, beef or cheese and spices and smothered with a tomato or chilli sauce before baking. Cheryl Jamison and I spent hours making these and ended up eating them cold, but they were delicious even then.

For the filling:

750 g/1 1/2 lb Monterey Jack or mozzarella cheese, grated

750 g/1 1/2 lb red Cheddar or other brightly coloured cheese

vegetable oil for frying

12–16 corn tortillas

Hatch Green Chilli Sauce (page 119)

To serve:

grated Cheddar or Monterey Jack cheese

chopped tomato

sliced spring onions

soured cream mixed with finely chopped fresh coriander

chopped ripe avocado (optional)

Pre-heat the oven to 180°C/350°F/Gas 4.

Grease a medium baking dish. Mix the cheeses with the onions in a bowl. Heat up 1–2.5 cm/1/2–1 inch oil in a small skillet or frying pan until the oil ripples with heat. Using tongs, dunk a tortilla in the oil long enough for it to go limp (a matter of seconds). Don't let the tortilla turn crisp. Repeat with the remaining tortillas and drain them of oil.

Still using the tongs, dip a tortilla in the chilli sauce to coat it lightly. Place the tortilla flat on a plate. Sprinkle with 3–4 tablespoons of the cheese filling and roll it up snugly. Transfer the enchilada to the baking dish and repeat the whole process with the remaining tortillas and fill- ing. Top the enchiladas with the remaining chilli sauce, making sure each one is well covered.

Bake in the oven for 15–20 minutes. Serve hot, sprinkled with gener- ous amounts of the suggested garnishes.

Lucky Corn

The Amerindian word *maiz* for corn means "sacred mother" or "giver of life", that is why legend has it that any corn wastefully scattered on the ground will go and complain to God. The inference is to bring retribution on the culprit. Alternatively, for luck, you could sprinkle cornmeal across your doorway to keep out enemies.

Elia's Chiles Rellenos

SERVES 4-6

I've renamed my own version of this dish in honour of the beautiful Elia Sanchez from Red Doc Farm in Belen, New Mexico. She makes a mean *chiles rellenos*. Elia mixes her batter differently with 3 egg whites, salt and a tablespoon or so of plain flour, but otherwise her version is the same as mine. She gave me some to try and they were sensational.

12 Anaheim or poblano chillies

vegetable oil for frying

¼ teaspoon salt

3 teaspoons white wine vinegar

500 g/1 lb Cheddar or Monterey Jack cheese

175 g/6 oz plain flour

1 teaspoon salt

1 teaspoon sugar

2 teaspoons baking powder

3 large eggs

1 teaspoon oil

375 ml/12 fl oz iced water

green or red enchilada sauce

The day before you need them, prepare the chillies by blistering them in very hot oil for 3–4 seconds at a time on each side. Quickly remove them with a slotted spoon and drop them into very cold water. Peel off the skins with your fingers, taking care not to remove the stalks. Leave the stalks on the chillies, but slit each chilli vertically along its side and remove all the seeds and veins (this makes the chillies less hot). Put the chillies in 600 ml/1 pint water mixed with the salt and vinegar and leave overnight.

If you prefer, you can blister each chilli for a few seconds at a time in the flames of a gas hob, turning the chilli constantly with a pair of tongs to ensure even blistering. Cool a little, but peel off the skins when the chillies are still reasonably hot, because it's easier then. Soak as above.

The next day, carefully rinse each chilli in cold water and gently pat dry with paper towels. Cut the cheese into strips the same length as the chillies and stuff each chilli with a piece of cheese. Keep the stuffed chillies cool in the refrigerator.

Sift together the flour, salt, sugar and baking powder into a mixing bowl. Beat the eggs, oil and iced water together and add to the flour mixture to form a batter. Use immediately.

Heat oil (at least 5 cm/2 in deep) in a frying pan. Dip the chillies one at a time in the batter, tap off the excess on the side of the bowl and carefully slide each battered chilli into the hot oil to brown, for about 2–3 minutes on each side. Cook in small batches only. Drain on paper towels. Serve immediately, accompanied by enchilada sauce.

Hatch Green Chilli Sauce

MAKES ABOUT 1 LITRE/2 PINTS

Hatch is a small New Mexican town in the southern Rio Grande Valley near Las Cruces. It carries the title of "green chilli capital of the world" because Hatch green chillies are considered *the best* by New Mexicans.

3 tablespoons vegetable oil

1 large onion, peeled and chopped

3 garlic cloves, peeled and finely chopped

2 tablespoons plain flour

500 g/1 lb mild Hatch green chillies, roasted, peeled and finely chopped

500 ml/16 fl oz chicken stock

1 teaspoon salt

1 teaspoon ground coriander

Heat up the oil in a heavy-based skillet or frying pan and sauté the chopped onion on medium heat until they soften, about 5–7 minutes. Stir in the garlic and continue to sauté for a further 2 minutes. Blend in the flour, lower the heat and continue cooking for another 2–3 minutes.

Stir in the chillies, stock and seasonings. Increase the heat and bring the mixture to a boil, then lower the heat to a simmer and cook until the sauce thickens, about 15-20 minutes. The sauce should be thick but still pourable . . . just. Serve as you wish, with other dishes.

Variation

For an interesting alternative flavour, you can add 6 chopped tomatillos, 3 chopped spring onions, 1 tablespoon chopped fresh coriander, 1 teaspoon ground cumin, 1 teaspoon dried Mexican oregano and 1 teaspoon freshly ground black pepper to the onions and garlic and sauté as above, then use half white wine and half chicken stock.

Chillies

Chillies are now eaten in every region of the United States and their popularity is still growing. Chilli pepper is the world's most popular spice — more is eaten in greater quantities than any other seasoning in the world. Chillies belong to the pod-bearing capsicums, members of the nightshade family, which also includes tomatoes, potatoes, aubergines and tobacco.

Chimayó Red Chilli Sauce

MAKES ABOUT 1 1ITRE/2 PINTS

At Chimayó I found a neat but productive and innovative little family factory called "Leona's Foods inc". This, I discovered, is the factory for the most amazingly flavoured tortillas – spinach, tomato, garlic, red chilli, jalapeño and pesto, sweet chocolate, butterscotch, cinnamon, banana, apple, blueberry and rum, and even fat-free tortillas are all made here. Unreal, I'm in seventh heaven. And to cap it all, their chilli peppers are good too.

2 tablespoons vegetable oil

1 medium onion, peeled and finely chopped

3 garlic cloves, peeled and finely chopped

180 g/6 oz ground dried red Chimay, chopped

1 litre/2 pints water or beef or vegetable stock, or half wine and half stock

1 teaspoon dried oregano, preferably Mexican

1 teaspoon salt

Heat the oil in a heavy-based saucepan, add the chopped onion and garlic and sauté until the onion is translucent and limp. Stir in the chilli followed by the water a little at a time. Finally, stir in the oregano and salt. Bring the sauce to a rolling boil, then reduce the heat to low and simmer for about 25–30 minutes. When cooked and ready, the sauce should be thick enough to thickly coat the back of a spoon. Serve warm to hot. If kept refrigerated, this sauce will last 5–6 days, or it can be frozen.

Guacamole Sanchez Style

SERVES 4–6

On Red Doc Farm in Belen, New Mexico, everyone cooks. From the littlest son to the oldest. This family is the epitome of "the family that eats together, stays together". To be around the Sanchez family and to hear them discuss their horse Cookie you get the feeling that their warmth even spills over onto their farm animals. I got to ride on Cookie, a gentle, intelligent grey horse who inspires confidence, even in a novice rider. I survived long enough to be pampered with this creamy "to-die-for" guacamole, made by the three youngest family members, Scoot, Florian and Emilio.

3 large ripe avocados

2 tablespoons fresh lime juice

2 medium ripe but firm tomatoes, finely diced

2 jalapeño peppers, de-seeded and very finely chopped

I green chilli, de-seeded and very finely chopped

250 g/8 oz soft Philadelphia cheese, or 60 ml/2 fl oz mayonnaise

½ teaspoon garlic salt

salt and pepper to taste

corn chips, to serve

Cut open the avocados and remove the stones. Cut the avocado into small cubes and put them in a large bowl. Add half the lime juice and mash. Add the remaining ingredients (except the corn chips) and continue mashing until smooth and creamy. Transfer to a serving dish and serve with corn chips, or as a sandwich filling.

Elia's Sopaipillas

MAKES 12

Sopaipillas are a form of lightweight flat bread often eaten in New Mexico, either savoury or sweet according to personal preference. When I first met "Doc" Roland Sanchez's mother, her first words after the initial hello were, "I hear you are making the sopaipillas with Elia, my daughter-in-law. They are my favourites, I can't wait!" And so it was that I helped Elia make lots of sopaipillas for that afternoon's family celebrations, a wedding anniversary and a birthday both on the same day.

500 g/1 lb plain flour

1/2 teaspoon baking powder

1/2 teaspoon salt

1/2 teaspoon sugar

1 1/2 teaspoons corn or vegetable oil

1 tablespoon evaporated milk

2 tablespoons warm water

corn or vegetable oil for deep-frying

maple syrup, sugar syrup or warmed and runny honey, to serve

Mix together the flour, baking powder, salt and sugar in a large mixing bowl. Make a well in the middle, pour in the oil, evaporated milk and warm water and stir together to form a smooth dough. This will be a little sticky, but cover your hands and a pastry board with some flour so you can handle the dough easily. Pick up the dough, rest it on the floured board and knead it vigorously until soft, about 1–2 minutes. Return the dough to the bowl, cover and leave to rise in a nice warm place (not the oven) for 20–30 minutes.

Pinch off pieces of dough and roll into about 12 separate balls. Arrange on a floured tray or plate, cover with a damp cloth and leave to prove for 20–30 minutes.

Heat oil for deep-frying and while it is heating, roll out each dough ball on the floured board to a circle measuring about 25 cm/10 inches in diameter and 5 mm/1/4 inch thick. Divide each circle into quarters and roll each quarter out again: this helps it puff up easily. (I learnt that little tip from Elia, so I'm passing it on to you too.)

Fry each quarter in the hot oil, carefully spooning the oil over the sopaipilla during frying so that it cooks and puffs up evenly. Cook for about 15–20 seconds each side so the browning is also even. When ready, lift out of the oil with a slotted spoon and drain on paper towels. Serve hot, with syrup or honey drizzled over the top.

Mango Chimichangas

SERVES 4–6

Although chimichangas are said to have originated in Arizona, I suspect they have now become a united taste of America, eaten throughout the States because of their deliciousness. You can actually create your own fillings – that's part of the fun of preparing this dish.

8 ripe mangoes, peeled and and diced, stones discarded

3 tablespoons caster sugar

3 tablespoons Cointreau or mango liqueur

juice of 2 large limes

3 teaspoons butter

125 g/4 oz toasted ground almonds

6 thin flour tortillas (20 cm/8 inches in diameter)

vegetable oil for deep-frying

125 g/4 oz icing sugar

thick whipped cream

2 tablespoons very finely grated orange zest, soaked in 2 tablespoons Cointreau

Put the diced mango in a heavy-based saucepan together with the caster sugar, alcohol and half the lime juice. Bring to a boil. Lower the heat and cook on medium, stirring all the time, until fruit is soft, pulpy and syrupy. Stir in the butter, almonds and remaining lime juice. Set aside to cool. Dry-heat the tortillas under the grill or in a dry skillet or frying pan to soften them and make them malleable. Keep the first batch of tortillas warm in a sealed plastic bag while you cook the rest. When ready, take out one tortilla at a time, spread it out on a plate and place spoonfuls of the mango filling in the centre. Fold the tortilla sides inwards, then roll the tortilla up into a tight package to enclose the filling. Secure with wooden cocktail sticks. Repeat the process with remaining tortillas and filling until all are used up.

Pour enough oil for deep-frying into a deep heavy-based saucepan, skillet or frying pan. The oil should be about 5 cm/2 inches deep. Heat the oil on medium heat until it just begins to crackle and smoke a little. Very carefully lower in 2–3 chimichangas (depending on the diameter of your pan) and fry them until they are light golden, about 2–3 minutes depending on how hot the oil is. Remove from the oil when golden and drain on paper towels. Serve immediately, topped with whipped cream and liqueur-soaked orange zest.

Agua Frescas

Basically, *agua frescas* are puréed, very ripe fruit blended with chilled water and crushed ice. A refreshing drink on hot days, but I have a personal tip to pass on to fellow "chilli heads". I know the temptation is to take mouthfuls of cold drinks like this when chilli is burning in your mouth. Please don't, you'll make it worse. I find cold drinks aggravate the situation. The thing I do is have a hot drink, as hot as my mouth can tolerate. Without fail, the burning stops like magic. Try it and leave beautiful refreshing drinks like this for days when you can actually taste what you are drinking. To make *agua frescas*, use any very ripe fruits, peel them and blend them together with iced water and crushed ice. The more fruit you use, the sweeter your drink.

Margarita

SERVES 2

This Mexican cocktail is made with tequila, lime juice, sugar and Triple Sec. Tequila comes from the starchy root of a plant known as blue agave. There is good tequila and there is mediocre tequila. The best I've ever tasted was made with *añejo* or old tequila, poured by my friend Mark Miller, at the Cayote Café. The two Marks, Miller and Kiffen, head honchos at the café treated me to typical Southwestern hospitality . . . lots of good food, served with style, and all washed down with excellent tequila.

1 wedge of lime (limón)

saucer of fine salt

30 ml/1 fl oz lime juice, from made with key limes (limón)

125 ml/4 fl oz premium silver tequila

60 ml/2 fl oz Triple Sec

lots of crushed ice

Chill 2 glasses in the freezer for about 30 minutes.

Run the wedge of lime around the rims of the chilled glasses to moisten them. Dip the rim of each glass upside down into the saucer filled with salt until the rims look lightly frosted.

Combine the lime juice, tequila, Triple Sec and crushed ice in a cocktail shaker and shake well to thoroughly mix the drink.

Carefully pour into the glasses and drink.

The First Margarita

The true origins of this popular Mexican cocktail had eluded me until recently when I came across this colourful story in "The Border Cookbook" by Cheryl and Bill Jamison. A certain barman, Francisco "Pancho" Morales from the city of Juárez, invented the Margarita on July 4th 1942. Pancho claimed a woman wandered into his bar and ordered a *magnolia*, a gin cocktail. He didn't know what it was, but being smart, he made up a Mexican substitute based on tequila. He called it *margarita*, the Spanish word for daisy.

Rain of Gold Punch

MAKES 2 LITRES/4 PINTS

1 litre/2 pints "rough" cider (scrumpy)

375 ml/12 fl oz brandy

pared zest and juice of 2 lemons

pared zest and juice of 4 oranges

1–2 tablespoons sugar

375 ml/12 fl oz sparkling apple juice, ginger ale or water

crushed ice

Combine all the ingredients in a large punch bowl, mix well and serve cold.

Native American **Tastes**

A meeting with a local fish called "Sucker" in Ashland, Winsconsin

Every year on the last Thursday in November, Americans sit down with their family and friends to a dinner that has become almost more popular than their next traditional feast a month later, Christmas Day. Thanksgiving is unique to America, and for most of its citizens, it is the feast which celebrates being an American, regardless of whether he or she has origins in Europe, Africa or other far-flung parts of the world. As they dine "upon turkey with cornbread stuffing, cranberry sauce, succotash, corn-on-the-cob, sweet potato casserole, stewed squash and tomatoes, baked beans with maple syrup, pecan pie and after-dinner chocolates", how many Americans today remember that a part of the thanks they are traditionally giving is to the Native Americans? To the many tribes right across America who introduced them to so many of the ingredients in their cuisine today, and much of the menu for this annual feast?

Long before Columbus or the Pilgrim Fathers arrived on their shores, the Native Americans had developed an enormous larder of nutritious foods and medicinal plants. Although not always entirely welcoming of the strangers who arrived in their midst, the Native American was prepared not only to share his natural resources, but also to teach the newcomers how to live off the land and to cultivate indigenous staples such as corn, squash and beans. Many settlers were slow learners, unused to working the land and afraid of the wild, and to them inhospitable land, which appeared to stretch endlessly into vast tracts of forest, prairie, desert and swamps.

One could make an entire television series and write numerous books about Native American cuisine and culture. Although I saw the signs of Native American influence in most of the different communities and states that I visited, I was only able to actually visit and film with one community – the Ojibwe or Chippewa in the northern state of Wisconsin. It is these people and their traditional food that I will be featuring in this chapter.

Before the arrival of Europeans, the traditional diet for most Northern Native Americans was wild game, fish, roots, nuts and berries harvested from the forests and lakes where they lived. There were two main groups. The Iroquois were hunters and farmers with well-organized and settled communities. They hunted and trapped animals for fur, which they traded with the French settlers in the North who had established trading posts around the Great Lakes, including Lake

Superior. There were also the Algonquin people, who included the Ojibwe tribes. They were primarily hunters and gatherers, though they did practise some farming. These communities moved from place to place, setting up camps and collecting foods as they appeared in every season. In early spring they tapped the maple trees for the sap, which they boiled down into a rich, sweet amber syrup. They moved through the woodlands, foraging for wild strawberries, ginger and other wild roots, and edible greens such as wild spinach, dandelion, watercress and edible fungi. They planted corn, squash, pumpkin and beans, which they harvested throughout the summer. In the autumn, they found numerous nuts and berries, especially cranberries, hazelnuts, acorns, elderberries and blue-berries. They dried the fruits and stored the nuts; they also dried or smoked the fish and meat for the long cold winters.

The most important, and nowadays unique, food enjoyed by the Ojibwe people is their wild rice, which they harvest from the lakes at the end of August and beginning of September. Many families still harvest the rice in the traditional way; in fact, they are the only people allowed to do so. *Mahnomin* (the Ojibwe name for wild rice) is extremely nutritious and has a delicious, slightly nutty flavour. It is not real-ly a rice at all, but a water grass that grows in the shal-lows of the lakes. When the rice is ripe, the Ojibwe go out in canoes in couples. While the man poles through the high grass, the woman holds an armful of stalks over the canoe and beats it with wooden sticks so that the ripe kernels fall into the bottom of the boat. Many seeds fall into the water and ensure a crop for the following year. When the canoe is full, the rice is brought ashore and laid out to dry in the sun. The dry husks are then loosened by pounding with sticks in a barrel or tub. When it has been winnowed, it is "trodden" in by men and then stored in bags made of bark, where it will keep through the following year until another harvest. The Ojibwe boil the wild rice

Fishing is child's play! Here with Native American kids on the shores of Lake Superior, Winsconsin

over slow fires with an infinite variety of ingredients. It can be eaten with venison, fish, bear meat, wild fowl such as duck and goose, it can even be ground into a flour for bread, and mixed with maple syrup and berries for delicious puddings. Wild rice has recently become very fashionable and can be bought in super-markets all over America and parts of Europe. There are large commercial plantations or rice paddies and mechanized harvests in Wisconsin and Minnesota, but the Ojibwe people still practise their own method and produce, I think, a superior rice.

The Northern Native Americans had some fasci-nating and unique cooking methods. For example, they would place stones, heated in the fire, in deep pits to slow-cook pots of beans simmered with mus-tard seed, maple syrup and meat. They made corn-bread by spreading the dough on a board or the blade of a hoe and placing it beside the fire to bake, known by the early settlers as hoe cakes. Bannocks, johnnycakes, ash cakes and pones were some of the breads and cakes that were made to take on journeys while out hunting or moving camp. The classic clam bake, so loved by Americans, is a Native American method of cooking fish by the same "hot stone in a pit" method – though often in sand rather than earth. A thick layer of seaweed is put over the hot stones and then layers of lobsters, clams, potatoes, corn husks, oysters, mackerel or cod and other seafood is covered over with a final layer of seaweed and wet animal hide or canvas weighted with stones on top. The whole lot is then left to steam gently until cooked. Some larger fish were "planked" by being stretched over a piece of wood or impaled on sticks and stuck in the ground close to the flame. They were then turned as they cooked.

Ojibwe history appears to have been relatively peaceful compared to that of other tribes. As was common practice in the 1820s, the US War Office appointed an agent to oversee the Ojibwe communities. One of these agents was called Henry R Schoolcraft. He married an Ojibwe woman and wrote extensively about his travels and experiences, which might have long passed into obscurity, had not the poet Longfellow based his epic poem "Hiawatha" on Schoolcraft's writings.

The Ojibwe are very serious about their environ-

ment. Their culture and daily lives are so closely bound up with the natural world around them that their knowledge of, and spiritual relationship with, the environment is now increasingly regarded with great respect by everyone, particularly those involved in environmental issues. They hold regular traditional feasts and powwows – times for wearing elaborate outfits made out of animal skins that were hunted in the winter for food, with deer hair, porcupine quills and dancing to imitate animals and the movement of grass and trees in the wind. There is singing, story-telling and feasting. The feasts include all the foods sacred to the tribe, such as berries of all kinds, wild meats, wild rice, wild potatoes and their own cultivated corn.

The Ojibwe people have a great sense of humour. They love to tell stories that make people laugh, as well as encourage them to understand what is growing and living all around them in "the Great Spirit's garden".

Shelly Bean teaches me the fine art of Native American barbecue on the shores of Lake Superior

Wild Rice and Venison Soup

SERVES 4–6

Wild rice is a sacred food, which the Ojibwe or Anishinabe call *mahnomin*. The rice is both culturally signifi-cant and an important staple of the Native American diet around the Northwest region of America. Jim St Arnold, an Ojibwe from Michigan, made me this soup and then told me his version of the wild rice legend. Centuries ago, their medicine men or spiritual leaders dreamt that their people must follow the great god "megasha" or "powisha" until they came to the place where food grew on water. The people packed their belongings and journeyed until they came upon wild rice growing in the rivers and lakes as seeds of the water grass. They knew then that they had arrived home, and so they stayed.

1 kg/2 lb minced venison

2 onions, peeled and finely diced

90 g/3 oz butter

2 litres/4 pints vegetable stock or water

salt to taste

3 carrots, cleaned and sliced into thin rounds

2 large red-skinned potatoes, washed and diced unpeeled

3 celery sticks, sliced into small pieces

250 g/8 oz wild rice

Combine the venison, onions and butter in a heavy-based saucepan or casserole dish and brown the meat on medium heat, about 20–25 minutes. Add the stock or water and season to taste. Stir in the carrots, potatoes and celery, partially cover the pan and allow to simmer on medium heat until the vegetables are almost soft, about 10 minutes.

Rinse the wild rice a couple of times in cold water to wash off any husks and debris. Drain the rice and add to the soup. Cover and simmer for 20–30 minutes or until the rice is cooked and the meat is tender. Taste and adjust seasoning. Serve hot, with Ojibwe Fry Bread (page 138) or by itself.

Ojibwe Squash and Corn Chowder

SERVES 4–6

Corn, beans and squash are often referred to as "the three sisters" by Native Americans. Much of the Native American diet is determined by seasonal availability of produce, but corn is the single most precious and versatile food that Native Americans ever bestowed upon America, and subsequently the rest of the world.

1 kg/2 lb lean pork, diced

1 large onion, peeled and very finely chopped

salt and pepper to taste

2 litres/4 pints water or vegetable stock

4 fresh ears of corn or 500 g/1 lb frozen sweetcorn kernels

500 g/1 lb butternut squash or pumpkin, peeled and cubed

Put the pork and chopped onion in a large saucepan or casserole dish. Sprinkle with ½ teaspoon salt and dry-cook, stirring all the time, for about 3–4 minutes on medium heat. This will "seal" the meat. Add the stock and simmer on a medium heat.

If using fresh corn, peel and discard the husks and silks, then rinse the corn thoroughly. Cut each ear of corn crosswise in half so that each piece can stand upright on the cut side. Rest each half cut-side down on a chopping board then, holding firmly and cutting as close to the cob as possible, slice off sections of the kernels at a time. Turn the cob round as you go until all the kernels are cut off. Take care not to include any part of the fibrous cob with the kernels. Save the corn kernels and discard the naked cob.

Add the kernels to the pork mix in the saucepan. Stir and add the squash or pumpkin as well. Continue to simmer on medium heat until the pork is soft and cooked and all the vegetables are cooked, about 30 minutes. The liquid should have reduced by at least one-third.

The soup can be served as it is, but if you prefer you can remove all the pieces of pork and purée the liquid in a blender or food processor, then reheat the puréed liquid in the pan together with the pork. Before serving, taste and adjust seasoning. Serve hot, with Ojibwe Fry Bread (page 138).

Wild Duck with Cranberries and Wild Rice Stuffing

SERVES 4–6

Wild ducks go well with wild rice, but the wild duck is leaner than the domestic variety so it is important to keep it covered with foil for the most part of the cooking, and to baste it two or three times to ensure it stays moist.

125 g/4 oz cranberries

250 ml/8 fl oz cranberry juice

125 ml/4 fl oz maple syrup

250 g/8 oz wild rice

750 ml/1 1/4 pints water

4 garlic cloves, peeled and very finely chopped

1 tablespoon paprika

2 teaspoons salt

2 teaspoons freshly ground black pepper

1 wild duck (about 2 kg/4 lb), cleaned

2 tablespoons corn or vegetable oil

1 medium onion, peeled and finely chopped

2 shallots or spring onions with green tops, finely chopped

125 g/4 oz pecans

Mix together the cranberries, cranberry juice, maple syrup, wild rice and half the water in a heavy-based saucepan. Bring to a boil on high heat. Reduce the heat to between low and medium, cover and steam the rice for about 40 minutes, until it is soft and cooked and all the water is absorbed. Throughout the cooking, add small amounts of the remaining water and stir from time to time to ensure the rice does not burn because of the syrup. Once cooked, allow to cool.

Pre-heat the oven to 180°C/350°F/Gas 4.

Mix together half the garlic with half the paprika and the salt and pepper. Rub this all over the duck, well into its cavity and as much under the skin flaps as possible. Rest the bird in a lightly greased large roasting tin.

In a skillet or frying pan, heat up the corn oil and fry the onion, shallots and remaining garlic on medium heat, stirring all the time, until soft and translucent. Add the remaining paprika and the pecans and cook for about 1 minute, stirring all the time. Stir in the rice mixture. Stuff this mixture into the duck, taking care not to pack it too tightly. Save any remaining rice mixture.

Cover the roasting tin with foil and bake for 1 hour. Remove the foil and lift up the bird, then spread any remaining rice mixture evenly in the tin. Place the bird on top and continue roasting for another 35–40 minutes to brown and crisp the skin. Serve hot, with baked sweet potatoes and steamed corn-on-the-cob cut into pieces of manageable size.

Venison Jerky

The winters in the American Northeast can be killers. Venison, like most of the meat and food of the region, is seasonal, so ways had to be devised to preserve food throughout the year. This is one of the many ways of ensuring a regular supply of venison.

1 kg/2 lb lean venison (hind quarter), semi-frozen so it is easy to cut

1 tablespoon Liquid Smoke (or mix hickory seasoning with soy sauce for a similar effect)

125 ml/4 fl oz Worcestershire sauce

250 ml/8 fl oz soy sauce

2 cloves garlic, crushed

3 teaspoons freshly ground black pepper

Using a sharp knife, cut the venison into long thin strips along the grain of the meat. Combine all the ingredients for the marinade in a large container which has a firm lid. Add the venison strips and stir well to coat all the venison pieces with marinade. Cover and refrigerate for 8-12 hours. Stir the meat periodically to ensure even seasoning.

Carefully and thoroughly line the bottom of the oven with foil to catch excess moisture.

Lift out the marinated strips of venison from the container and shake off the excess marinade. Carefully arrange the strips on the oven racks. Turn the oven on to 110°C/225°F/Gas 1/4 and slowly cook the meat for 4 hours. Turn each strip carefully, return the racks to the oven and cook for a further 4 hours.

The meat should be desiccated and firm to the touch to confirm it is well cooked. Turn off the oven and allow the meat to cool completely, then remove it from the racks and store in airtight containers in the refrigerator or in a cool place until needed.

You will need to rehydrate the meat by cooking or soaking it in lots of stock, broth or water for a few fours before using it in cooking.

Venison and Wild Rice Casserole

SERVES 4–6

The deer season was starting and we were invited to a sumptuous venison and wild rice feast by Jim Arnold and his stunning fiancée Judy. She told me that Jim often cooked for her, but he had never cooked this particular recipe, even though he'd promised her many times. She saw our visit as a good excuse as any for him to shine – and shine he did, with fresh venison.

500 ml/16 fl oz water

375 ml/12 fl oz cream of mushroom soup

90 g/3 oz wild mushrooms or button mushrooms

250 g/8 oz wild rice

6 lean venison chops

salt and pepper to taste

1 medium onion, peeled and thinly sliced into rounds

3 rashers of lean bacon

Pre-heat the oven to 180°C/350°F/Gas 4.

In a heavy-based casserole dish, mix the water and mushroom soup. Wash the mushrooms and add them to the dish. Rinse the wild rice in cold water a few times, drain and stir into the mixture. Spread the venison chops out in the sauce, season to taste and arrange the onion rings on top followed by the bacon. Cover and bake in the oven for about 1–1½ hours or until the meat and rice are soft and cooked. Serve hot, with fresh salad greens of your choice.

The Rice Harvest

Jim reckons there are only two kinds of people who eat wild rice, the rich because they can afford it, and his people, the Ojibwe, because they harvest it. Wild rice is the seed of a species of water grass, most common around the Midwest and the Great Lakes. The grass usually grows 60 cm–2 metres/2–6 feet deep, roots firmly embedded in the muddy bottoms of lakes and rivers. The rice is only harvested from mid-August to mid-September when it is mature, so as not to ruin future crops.

Fresh Roast Rabbit

SERVES 4–6

The Ojibwe did not believe in wanton waste of food. They believed – and still do – that everything has a life and a spirit. So one must say "thank you" to any animal that gives up its life for you to eat. Before gathering food from the wild, the Ojibwe offer a small piece of tobacco as thanks in the hope that the food will return again the following year. Wild life such as squirrel, raccoon, beaver, muskrat, porcupine, wild bear, wild duck and partridge are all a significant part of the Native American diet, and rabbits too are a part of that chain of abundance in the wilds.

I whole medium rabbit (1.5 kg/3 lb), skinned and well cleaned and washed

salt and pepper to season

2 tablespoons vegetable oil

2 large onions, peeled and sliced into rings

4 garlic cloves, peeled and finely chopped

4 medium potatoes, washed and halved unpeeled

6-8 medium carrots, cleaned and each cut into three

500 ml/16 fl oz water or vegetable stock or broth

Pre-heat the oven to 180°C/350°F/Gas 4.

Season the rabbit all over with some salt and pepper. In a large heavy-based skillet or frying pan, heat up the oil. Carefully place the rabbit in the hot oil and turning it regularly, quickly brown it on all sides, about 10–15 minutes on medium heat.

Remove the rabbit from the pan and place it in a greased baking dish or roasting tin. Surround with the cut vegetables, making sure some of them (especially the onions and garlic) are stuffed inside the rabbit as well as on the outside. Carefully pour in the water around the outer edge of the dish or tin. Sprinkle with some salt and pepper. Roast in the oven for about 1–1½ hours or until the rabbit and vegetables are all well cooked. Serve hot, with some wild rice.

What's In a Name?
O'Chipewa? O'Jibwa? Anishinabe? Which is it to be? I want to do the right thing. What is the correct name for, or way to address, the Native Americans I filmed in Minnesota? I posed my direct question to Jim and Judy St Arnold, Shelly Bean, Val Berber, Tom Thein and many other locals. Their explanation is that apparently, when Europeans first arrived in North America, this particular group of locals identified themselves as Ojibwe, but depending on whether the immigrant was French- or English-speaking they pronounced it differently. Over time, the "O" was lost from O'Chippewa and it became Chippewa and Ojibwe. Now the locals variously refer to themselves as either Anishinabe (pronounced ani-shinaa-bay) or Ojibwe (pronounced ojib-way).

Lake "Salmon" Fishboil with Vegetables

SERVES 4–6

We were catching fish on the shores of Lake Superior in Wisconsin. Or, more correctly, I was watching Dana Jackson haul in his catch – about twelve big fish in just two hours. I was impressed, but I could barely identify the variety of the catch, so I asked him to go through the names. "Pike, trout, walleye, salmon, sucker." "Sucker?" I asked, "What kind of fish is that?" He said, "Pick it up and check out its lips." I did, and what great kissers they were. A fish with the most kissable lips in the world. Dana then cooked us this salmon. It is a very simple dish, but it tastes sensational, especially if prepared on the beach straight after it is caught. An alternative way to cook it is to wrap the seasoned salmon in greased foil and bake it in the hot coals of your beach campfire. The vegetables can then cook in a pot on top of the fire.

3 litres/6 pints water for boiling

2 bay leaves

salt and pepper to taste

1 large freshwater salmon (about 2 kg/4 lb), gutted and cleaned

6 medium potatoes, peeled and halved

3 large onions, peeled and quartered

6 medium carrots, cleaned and topped and tailed

250 g/8 oz butter (optional)

Bring the water to a boil in a large cooking pot and add the bay leaves as you prepare your fish and vegetables. Lightly season the water as it boils.

Using a very sharp knife, cut the salmon into 2–3 large pieces. It is important not to cut the fish into small pieces because fresh fish cooks very fast and small pieces would disintegrate quickly in the cooking stock. Sprinkle salt and pepper all over the fish pieces, rubbing it all over, inside and out. Add the potatoes, onions and carrots to the boiling water and cook for about 20 minutes. Carefully add the pieces of salmon to the cooking vegetables and stock. Cook for a further 10–15 minutes or until everything is cooked and ready.

Using a slotted spoon, fish out and discard the bay leaves. Carefully remove the salmon and vegetables from the stock. Strain off most of the stock and serve as a light fish soup, but save enough stock to serve with the salmon and vegetables.

Divide the cooked salmon into appropriate portions for your guests and dot each piece with butter (if using) before serving. Serve hot, with the vegetables.

Succotash

SERVES 4–6

I have finally found the meaning of Succotash. I found it in *Blue Corn and Chocolate*, a book by Elizabeth Rozin in which she explains that succotash is actually a mis-pronunciation of a Native American word for a dish with a mixture of corn and beans. The word is *msickquatasch*. It is the sort of stew for which you can substitute any type of beans or peas to help transform leftovers into winners. To make a vegetarian version like the original Native American style, leave out the meat and possibly the cheese too. You can also stir in 250 g/8 oz plain yogurt.

4 tablespoons corn or vegetable oil

500 g/1 lb leansmoked hock, bacon or pork, cut into thick cubes

1 large onion, peeled and cut into short thin slices

3 garlic cloves, peeled and finely chopped

1 red and 1 green medium pepper (capsicums), de-seeded and chopped

1 kg/2 lb dried beans or peas of your choice, cooked and drained (e.g. red kidney or butter beans)

1.5 kg/3 lb sweetcorn kernels

375 ml/12 fl oz water

salt and pepper to taste

3 firm ripe tomatoes, de-seeded and cut into large cubes

150 g/5 oz Cheddar or Parmesan cheese, grated

In a heavy-based saucepan, heat up the oil and quickly brown the outside of the meat on high heat. Lower the heat and add the onion, garlic, peppers, beans, sweetcorn and water. Stir well, taste and season with salt and pepper. Simmer on low heat for 15 minutes, then add the cubed tomatoes. Continue to simmer for a further 20 minutes until the sauce has reduced. Sprinkle with the cheese and serve hot, with moulded steamed rice or by itself.

Ojibwe Wild Rice with Bacon

SERVES 2–3

Cecilia Ashmun of Wisconsin made this dish for me after she and her husband William had been showing me how they harvested the wild rice in mid-August. I'm sure I bored her thoroughly with my rice obsession, but she gave no indication. The next time I saw her, she had a surprise warm package for me. Kind warm-hearted Cecilia had cooked me one of her husband's favourite foods, wild rice with bacon. It is now going to be one of my favourites too.

60 g/2 oz butter, plus extra to serve (optional)

4 rashers of lean bacon, cut into small pieces

250 g/ 8 oz wild rice

750 ml/1 ¼ pints water or chicken or vegetable stock

salt to taste

parsley, to garnish (optional)

Wild rice takes a while to cook, but you can soak it in clear, clean water for up to 2 hours or even overnight (if you like your rice really soft) before using it in the recipe. Generally, the rule is 1 part wild rice to 3 parts water, but if you soak your rice first, you should reduce the volume of liquid by one-third, and you will need only half the amount of cooking time.

Melt the butter in a casserole dish or heavy-based saucepan and cook the bacon pieces on medium heat until they are cooked and slightly crunchy, about 4–5 minutes.

Rinse the wild rice a couple of times in cold water to wash off any husks and debris. Drain the rice and add it to the bacon in the pan. Stir in the water or stock, season to taste and bring to a boil. Lower the heat and simmer until all the water is absorbed and the rice is cooked, about 40 minutes. The grains should have burst open and be tender but not mushy.

Serve hot, fluffed up with some butter and garnished with parsley if you like. Serve by itself or as a dressing for meat, fish and other vegetable dishes.

Squash with Maple Syrup and Nut Butter

SERVES 4–6

Squash is another sacred staple food for Native Americans from both North and South America. With corn and beans, it is one of "the three sisters" of Native American cuisine. If you like, you can use honey instead of maple syrup.

2–3 medium yellow squash

250 ml/8 fl oz water, mixed with 1 tablespoon maple syrup

90 g/3 oz almond, pine nut or hazelnut butter

90 g/3 oz maple syrup

3 tablespoons very finely chopped parsley

1 teaspoon ground allspice

Pre-heat the oven to 180°C/350°F/Gas 4.

Cut each squash in half, clean and discard the seeds and other debris, wash thoroughly and pat dry with paper towels. Arrange the squash halves face down in a casserole dish and pour the water and maple syrup mixture around them. Bake in the oven for 30–40 minutes or until soft to the touch.

Turn the squash over into their correct positions and spoon the nut butter, maple syrup, parsley and allspice into the partly cooked squash. Using oven gloves or a cloth to hold the squash, carefully swirl each squash gently around so that the inside gets well coated with the mixture.

Bake for another 30 minutes before serving hot, with either roast pheasant, wild duck or venison.

Ojibwe Fry Bread

MAKES 20–24 PIECES

Alright, so it's confession time, this stuff is addictive. It is served with just about every meal you order out. I first got hooked when I ate my first fry bread at a Native American powwow near Bayfield in Wisconsin. A powwow, for those who are not sure, is a Native American periodic get-together. It is for bonding and sharing in an atmosphere of mutual trust amid ceremonial rights, music, masses of food and some serious dancing. It is a time to wear and display full tribal regalia. It has great atmosphere for families, friends and everyone. What I found out first hand is that it also has an atmosphere charged with emotion and a need to eat. So I ate and ate and ate lots of *zaasakokwaan*, as the Ojibwe call fry bread.

1.25 kg/2½ lb plain flour, sifted, plus extra for kneading

60 g/2 oz butter, melted

2 large eggs

625 ml/21 fl oz milk or water

3 teaspoons baking powder

vegetable oil for deep-frying

Blend all the ingredients together in a large mixing bowl to form a sticky dough. Add small portions of extra flour and knead on a floured pastry or chopping board until the dough is no longer sticky. Form the dough into small balls according to the number of portions wanted, in this case 20–24, then shape them into fingers.

Heat up some oil in a deep skillet or frying pan and deep-fry the bread fingers in small batches until all are cooked through and golden. Remove from the oil and drain on paper towels. Keep warm in a low oven until all are fried. Serve hot, as you wish.

Hoe Cakes

SERVES 4–6

Hoe cakes are basically unleavened loaves of cornbread. They are usually baked on an outside fire of some sort, either on or near a campfire or in the fields. I've heard a few explanations as to how the cakes got their name, but the following stories are my favourites. One is that the old Indians taught the early European immigrant settlers how to make and cook these cakes around the campfire using work hoes as racks or baking tins. The other is that the black slaves of the South turned their field hoes into culinary implements and improvised an ingenious way to cook cornbread while working in the fields. Whichever is correct, the fact is that hoe cakes are good and tasty. Today, they are more like griddle cakes.

500 ml/16 fl oz water

250 g/8 oz cornmeal (polenta)

125 g/4 oz plain flour

1 teaspoon salt

2 teaspoons baking powder

**750 ml/1 1/4 pints equal parts milk
and water**

butter or vegetable oil, for cooking

Make a batter with the ingredients.

Butter or oil a hot griddle. Drop large tablespoonsful of the batter on to the griddle. Cook until golden. Turn and cook the other side.

Wild Rice and Berries

SERVES 8–10

Jim St Arnold made up this dessert using two of the tribe's sacred foods, wild rice and berries. When I asked Jim what comments he wanted me to write for his original pudding, he said, "Dorinda says it's good". So here it is, and I stand by my original assessment.

250 g/8 oz wild rice

250 g/8 oz cranberries

750 ml/1¼ pints water

125 g/4 oz each of blueberries and raspberries

250 ml/8 fl oz maple syrup

2 teaspoons ground cinnamon

250 ml/8 fl oz thick whipped cream, to serve (optional)

Rinse the wild rice a couple of times in cold water to wash off any husks and debris. Drain the rice and put it into a heavy-based saucepan. Add the cranberries and water and bring to a boil. Lower the heat to medium and cook for about 30 minutes or until the rice grains cook and burst open. Stir in the blueberries, raspberries and maple syrup. Allow to cook for a further 5–10 minutes before you stir in the cinnamon. Mix together well, remove from the heat and serve hot, with or without cream.

Lag or Lagilette

SERVES 6–8

The first time I had this was on the shores of Lake Superior, Wisconsin, at a campsite with Shelly Bean and a few friends. I saw Shelly passing on her cooking skills to her 12-year-old daughter, Laura Wiggins. They were making "Lag" or "Lagilette", they told me. It is a skillet or fry-pan bread cooked very quickly in a deep cast-iron frying pan lined with greased aluminium foil. Laura placed the dough in the pan, covered it, and cooked it on the campfire. It was delicious. Like all good gourmets, you learn to cook what you like, so I asked for the recipe. With their permission, here it is.

500 g/1 lb plain flour

2 tablespoons baking powder

1 teaspoon salt

2 tablespoons sugar

125 g/4 oz butter, cut into small pieces

250 ml/8 fl oz milk or water

Mix all the dry ingredients together in a large mixing bowl, add the butter and milk or water and stir well to mix and form a dough. Flour a pastry board and knead out the dough, either by hand or preferably with a rolling pin, for about 15–20 minutes. Form into either 1 large ball or smaller balls.

Line a heavy-based cast-iron skillet or deep frying pan with foil, lightly grease the foil and place the formed dough ball(s) in it. Cover and bake on the grid of a hot campfire, or on top of your stove on medium to low heat, for about 20-30 minutes until cooked and golden brown. Turn the bread over halfway through cooking to brown both sides. Serve hot with butter, honey or gravy.

Na Puddin Shiminen

DUMPLINGS WITH BERRIES

SERVES 4–6

Val Barber of Lac Courte Oreilles Community makes this pudding. She calls it her summertime dish, because it evokes memories of growing up around her grandmother who made the pudding. She says the smell drove her and her siblings wild as they clamoured round their grandmother to eat it. She is right. Grown-ups though we are, my crew and I jostled over the pudding just like kids. It has that effect on you.

For the base:

I kg/2 lb blueberries

250 ml/8 fl oz maple syrup

250 ml/8 fl oz water

30 g/I oz unbleached plain flour

60 g/2 oz butter

For the pudding top:

500 g/I lb unbleached plain flour

1/2 teaspoon freshly grated nutmeg

4 tablespoons butter

250 ml/8 fl oz buttermilk

To serve:

375 ml/12 fl oz thick cream

125 g/4 oz sugar

Make the base: in a heavy-based saucepan, combine the blueberries, maple syrup, water, flour and butter and bring to a boil. Lower the heat to medium and cook for about 20–30 minutes or until the berries look mashed to a pulp. Do not stir too often.

Make the pudding top: sift all the dry ingredients together into a large mixing bowl, then rub in the butter by hand until well mixed. Make a well in the middle and pour in the buttermilk, a little at a time, stirring to mix with a fork as you go. Continue until all the milk is used up and the topping is thick, soft and sticky – but not too wet or dry. Turn the dough out onto a floured surface. Flour your hands and scoop out pieces of dough to form into balls about the size of squash balls. The dough should make about 12–14 balls. Flatten the balls a little on top to form thick patties. Arrange them carefully side by side on top of the blueberry mix to completely cover the surface area. Cover, lower the heat and continue to cook on the stove top for about 12–15 minutes. Do not remove the lid before then.

Whip up the thick cream and sugar. Once the pudding is ready and cooked, serve it hot, with the sweetened whipped cream.

Winter Green Tea

SERVES 4–6

Winter greens have tiny leaves (about the size of a thumb), which are slightly shiny. They grow wild in Minnesota. The young leaves are light green and pretty, but they turn a darker green as they mature. They taste like a cross between light mint and aniseed. Winter green tea is an infusion of the leaves only and is very refreshing. The tea is also medicinal and good for upset stomachs. Tom Thein, an Ojibwe from Ashland, Wisconsin, gave me his version of winter green tea after my crew and I shared a pot of it with him.

2 cups winter green leaves

½ cup mint leaves

just a handful of red clover blossoms (about 15)

2 litres/4 pints water

maple syrup or sugar to taste

Rinse the winter green leaves and the mint leaves in cold water to clean them. Check the red clover blossoms for insects. Dry the leaves with a clean tea towel and tear them into tiny pieces by hand. Place the torn leaves in a large saucepan and add the red clover blossoms. Boil the water and pour it over the leaves and blossoms. Steep for about 10–15 minutes; do not boil. Strain and serve warm to hot. The tea should not need sweetening if the clover blossoms are new, but you can add maple syrup or sugar to suit your personal taste.

Raspberry Stem or Leaf Tea

SERVES 4–6

Most of the "medicines" found in the forests and on the reservations double up as food and medicine. The Native American knowledge and usage of local vegetation goes back centuries, and I was glad to see so many young kids taking a keen interest in learning from their elders. Val Barber of Lac Courte Oreilles took me on a nature study tour of the reservation surrounding her house that forms part of a natural backyard for her. Val's knowledge and the variety of useful and edible plants was mind-boggling. I learnt heaps.

1 medium to large bunch of raspberry stems or leaves

1.5 litres/3 pints water

maple sugar, syrup or ordinary sugar

Clean the raspberry stems and check for any insects. Fold and tie with string into workable lengths to fit into a saucepan. Put the stems into the pan, pour the water over the top and bring to a boil.

Boil for about 5–10 minutes, then remove from heat and strain. Serve hot, with or without sweetening as you wish.

Index

African American cooks 24
  Tastes 23–29
Aghoitta alla Novello (stew with Fish
  Croquettes) 84
Agua Frescas (fruit drink) 123
Alligator Piquante 12
Almond
  Jelly 55
  Tea 54
Apple Strudel 67-68
Arcadians 7
Aztecs, Mexico 107-8

Beef and Asparagus in Black Bean Sauce
  45
Blue Corn Pancakes with Cider Syrup 113
Bratwurst in Ale 60
Bread
  and Potato Dumplings 64
  Pudding with Rum Sauce 21
Breads 21, 30, 64-5, 68, 138
  see also Cornbread
Burritos with Potato and Bacon 112

Cajun 7-8
  American Tastes 7-55
  cuisine 7-8
  Seafood Salad 18
cakes 69, 105, 139
Candied Yams 29
Catfish Pizzaiola 82
Cheesecakes 70, 103
Chicken
  and Andouille Sausage Gumbo 11
  Liver Pâté, Home-made 97
  Soup 91
  Southern Fried 26
  Steamed with Red Wolfberries 46-7
  Stuffed Breast of 77
Chilli 108-9
Chimayó Red Chilli Sauce 120
Chinese
  American culture 42
  American Tastes 40-55
  cookery books 41
  cooking methods 41-2
  cuisines 40
  dim sum 42
  Exlusions Act (1882) 41
  food 41
  "stir-frys" 42, 51
Cholent 93-4
  Kneidlach (Dumpling) 94
Cioppino 75
Clam
  Bake 127

Chowder, New England 76
Cocido 110
Codfish Balls
  or Cakes 85
  in Sauce 85
Coffee
  Iced 71
  Spiced 22
Collard Greens and Smoked Neck Bones
  33
Corinthian Mint Julep 38
Corn
  and Crab Bisque 10
  Soup 44
Cornbread
  à la Ernestine 32
  Dorinda's Sweet 31
  Hush Puppies (fritters) 19
Crawfish Boil 13-14
Creole cuisine 7

Dorinda's Cajun Combo Seasoning Mix 9
dumplings 64, 141

Elia's
  Chiles Rellenos 118
  Sopaipillas 122

Fish 13-14, 16, 25, 47, 76, 84, 100, 115, 134
  Blackened 14
  Chowder 76
Fillets in Wine Sauce 47
Fizzy Chocolate Milkshake 106
Fritto Misto di Pesce 80
Fruits
  Cold Soup 58
  drinks 71, 123
  Fried 55
  Punch 71
Funnel Cake 69

Gefilte Fish 100
German
  American recipes 57
  American Tastes 56-71
  cooking 56-7
  Potato Salad 63
  recipes 57
  settlers 56
    Minnesota 57
Green Chilli
  Enchiladas 117
  Hatch Sauce 119
  Soup 111
Green Cooler 22
Guacamole Sanchez Style 121

Heritagefest 57
Hoe Cakes 139
Honey Cake 105
Hoppel Poppel 59
Hoppin' John 34

Iced Tea 39
Italian
  American homes 74
  American Tastes 72-87
  communities 74
  confectionery businesses 73
  cuisine 72, 74
  immigrants 73
  regional cooking 72

Jewish
  Americans 90
    cuisine 88-90
    Tastes 88-106
  Drinks 106
  New Yorkers 88, 90

Kipling, Rudyard 57
Kneidlach (Matzah balls) 92
Knishes or Burekas 96-7
Kofta 95
Kosher
  foods 89
  laws 89-90
  religious observances 90
Kung Pao Prawns 50

Lag or Lagilette 140
Lake "Salmon" Fishboil with Vegetables 134
Lewis, Sinclair 57
Limeade/Limefizz 22
Lobster, Baked Stuffed 83
Longfellow, Henry, "Hiawatha" 127

Ma Po Tofu 48
Macaroni Cheese, Ultimate 27
Mango Chimichangas 123
Maple Syrup
  Chiffon Cake 105
  with Squash and Nut Butter 137
Margarita 124
Melon Shake 87
Mexican
  cuisine 109
  Indians 107

Na Puddin Shiminen (Dumplings with
  Berries) 141
Native Americans 125-6
  cooking methods 126-7

Native Americans *cont.*
  Tastes 125-43
  tribes 8
Navajo people 108
New England Clam Chowder 76
New Mexican 109
  barbecues 108
  Carne Adovada 114
  cuisine 108
  Tastes 107-24
New Orleans, Louisiana 7

Ojibwe
  community 125
  Fry Bread 138
  Squash and Corn Chowder 129
  tribes 126-7
  Wild Rice with Bacon 136
Okra and Seafood Gumbo 25
One Pot
  cooking 7-8
  Pork 28

Pain Perdu 20
Pea Soup 58
Peach Cobbler 35
Penn, William 56
Phyllis's Jambalaya 15
Pickled Herring and Potato Salad 102
Polenta 80
  with Quails 79
Pork
  Ribs and Sauerkraut 59
  Spareribs with Black Bean Sauce 49
Port Townsend Immigration Aid society 41
Potato
  Bread 65

Latkes 98
Salads 63, 102
Prawn Boulettes 16
Pueblo people 108

Quails with Polenta 79

Rabbit, Fresh Roast 133
Rain of Gold Punch 124
Raisin Syrup 106
Raspberry Stem or Leaf Tea 143
Red Cabbage 66
Rogue's Carnitas 116-17

Salads 18, 63, 102
Salmon
  à la Sea Breeze 99-100
  Lake, Fishboil with Vegetables 134
San Francisco
  Chinatown 40-2
  "Gateway to Asia" 40
Sauces 21, 47, 49, 85, 120
Sauerbraten 61
Sauerkraut Hot Dish 63
Savoiardi Delight 87
Savoury Potato Kugel 101
Schoolcraft, Henry R. 127
Seafood Chimichangas 115
Seafood Stock 10
Sephardi Jews 88, 90
Shoofly Pie 68
Sizzling Rice Soup 43
soups 43-4, 58, 111, 128
Sour Cream Topping 104
Southern cooking 24
Spaghetti alle Vongole 81-2
Spanish gastronomic influence 108

Spinach, Fresh, with Fermented Bean Curd
  54
Spoon Bread 30
Squash with Maple Syrup and Nut Butter
  137
Stir-Fried
  Bean Sprouts 52
  Chinese Green Vegetables 51
Stuffed Mushrooms 17
Succotash 135
Swabian Noodles 62
Sweet
  Noodle Kugel 104
  Potato and Pecan Pie 36-7

Teas 39, 46-7, 54, 142-3
Thanksgiving Day 125
Tomato Sauce 95
tortilla 109

Veal Parmigiana 78
Vegetarian Potstickers 53
Venison
  Jerky 131
  and Wild Rice Casserole 132
  and Wild Rice Soup 128

Wild Duck with Cranberries and Wild Rice
  Stuffing 130
Wild Rice
  and Berries 140
  stuffing 130
  and Venison Soup 128
Winter Green Tea 142

Zabaglione 86

Acknowledgements

I would like to thank the following people:

My publishers, Judith Curr at Ballantine, and Amelia Thorpe and Penny Simpson at Ebury Press.

Milton Wordley and his assistant James Knowler for the food photography.

Cath Kerry for the recipe testing and food styling for the photographs.

Researchers Helen Murray, Cassie Farrell, Valerie Haselton, Hatty Ellis, Kate Gough and Caroline Pringle.

Location photographers Cassie Farrell, Valerie Haselton and Nickki Colton.

Arlene Agus, Esther Winner, the Lubovitch Youth Organization of Brooklyn, Levana Kirschenbaum Michelle Topor, Marta Pace-Barker, Sefatia Romeo, Lena Novello and the Gloucester Fishermen's Wives Association, Reverend Tillman, James and Chaquita Riles and family, Juanita Dixon, Ernestine Myers and family, the congregation of the First African Baptist Church in Savannah, Georgia, Shirley Fong-Torres, Dorothy Quoc, the Sanchez family, the Wendinger family, Leo Berg, Jim St Arnold, Widley and Doris Herbert (Soop) and Family and Kurt and Kim Vorhies for their recipes and for their participation in the programme.

Alison Thomas and Sue Shephard, of Harvest Entertainment.